M000307951

We Invented the Wheel
Poems by Reesom Haile

ዕንክሊል

ቅሜጠ ግጥሚ ብዶ/ር ርእሶም ሃይለ

English Translations with
Charles Cantalupo

The Red Sea Press Inc.
Publishers & Distributors of Third World Books

P.O. Box 1982
Trenton, NJ 08607

RSP

P.O. Box 48
Asmara, ERITREA

The Red Sea Press Inc.

Publishers & Distributors of Third World Books

<u>P.O. Box 1982</u>      <u>P.O. Box 48</u>
Trenton, NJ 08607   Asmara, ERITREA

Copyright © 2002 Reesom Haile and Charles Cantalupo
First Printing 2002

Cover Illustration by Lawrence F. Sykes

Book Design: Getahun Seyoum Alemayehu
Cover Design: Ashraful Haque

Catalog-in-Publication Data available from Library of Congress

ISBN 1-56902-162-7 (Cloth)
ISBN 1-56902-162-5 (Paperback)

Acknowledgements

Poems from *We Invented the Wheel* have also appeared in *AI Performance, Asmarino.com, Dehai.org, Drunken Boat, Exquisite Corpse, Samizdat* and *Titanic Operas.*

For Peachy

We came close to her – so close,
We thought she'd stay,
And you wouldn't take her away,
Though she belonged to you.

ካብኻዶ ቀሪብናያ?
ዝወሰድካያ ናትካ እያ
መሲሉና ድኣ ኣይምሰልካ
ዘይተሕድግ እንኩ ምስ በልካ

TABLE OF CONTENTS
ትሕዝቶ

ix

x

xi

We Invented the Wheel
Poems by Reesom Haile

ዕንክልሊል

ቅሚጠ ግጥሚ ብዶ/ር ርእሶም ሃይለ

English Translations with
Charles Cantalupo

A Country

She lays her cool head
And warm feet
By the sea.
Small, self-made
Independent,
With a belly full of fire
And a big heart of wisdom,
She is blessed
With love and children.
I hear what she says
And rely on what she does,
Fierce as a tiger
With new cubs.

ሃገር እላ

ሃገር እላ
ገምገም ባሕሪ
እግራ ቄላ
ርእሳ ቝሪ
ንእስ ኢላ
ከብዳ ጓህሪ
ዕብይ ኢላ
ልባ ምኽሪ
ርእሳ ኽኢላ
ብናታ ጸዕሪ
አይ ብአፋን ብግብሪ
ፈጢሩላ
ምስ ደቃ ፍቕሪ
መን ክኽእላ
ሓራስ ነብሪ

Beyond

Beyond
Gold, wealth,
Riches, honors,
Status and the promise
Of paradise
After a lifetime of struggle
Our country is free.
Be happy.

ክንየው

ክንየው ሃብቲ
ክንየው ወርቂ
ክንየው ሽመት
ክንየው ጨርቂ
ክንየው ህይወት
ክንየው ጽድቂ
ደስ ዝብለኒ ብሓቂ
ድሕሪ ኽንደይ ጭንቂ
ናይ ዓደይ ነጻነት በርቂ

Drinking Independence

Thanks for your invitation
To eat and drink,
But I've drunk independence
Like pure water,
And I don't want to ruin the taste.

I've cupped my hands,
Used tin cans, bowls and spoons
And I've put my lips to the source –
Independence like pure water –
Drinking my fill.

Remembering
The home I had to abandon,
My fields gone to waste,
The bedrock I split
And independence like pure water

Bursting out,
I'm awake before the beggars
Start their daily rounds,
And I protect
My independence like pure water.

ጽሩይ ማይ ነጸነት

ጽሩይ ማይ ነጸነት ሰቲኻ
ብላዕ ስተ ንዝብለኻ
በሊዕ እንድየ!
ሰትየ እንድየ!
ጸጊበ እንድየ!
እንተበልካዮም
ሐቆኻ እንዲኻ ምኣስ ተጋሪኻ

ጽሩይ ማይ ነጸነት ሰቲኻ
ደለኻ ብኢድኻ
ደለኻ ብታኒካ
ደለኻ ብማንካ ሐንፈፍካ
ካልእ ማልእ ይትረፍካ ከይትጽይቕ ኣፍካ

ጽሩይ ማይ ነጸነት መን ወሃቢኻ?
ዓድኻ በረኻ በረኻ ዓድኻ
ደንጉላ ፈሊጽካ ፈንቂልካ
ዘንታዕካዮ ባዕልኻ

ሐሉ ሐደራኻ ሐሉ!
ጽሩይ ማይ ነጸነትካ ብጽሩዩ ክህሉ
ስለ ማርያም ንእኽሉ ከይሐርአሉ

7

An Eritrean Recipe

Take looking good
And standing tall.
Think and provide.
Make glad.
Self determine.
Believe and know,
Independent until death.
Time for the fire.
Braving all,
Throw in some sea salt
And berbere pepper.
More berbere.
Stirring often,
Cook and taste.
Is it good?
Whoa, brother!
Sister, that's Eritrean!

ኤርትራውነት

ካብ መልክዕ
ካብ ቁኑመት
ካብ ውሕልነት
ካብ ሕያውነት
ካብ እምነት
ካብ ፍልጠት
ካብ ጅግንነት
ካብ ቄራጽነት
ምሳኺ ሞተይ ነጺነት
ሓዊስካ አብ ሓዊ ትስኽትቶ

ጨው ትንስንሰሉ
በርበረ ትገብረሉ
በርበረ ትውሽኸሉ ተብስሉ

ኣኸሱ ተብሉ ትጥዕሞ!
ጌጋ ይኸልኣለይ እምበር
ሱስ ሓወይ ሓብተይ እንተቢሉካስ
ኤርትራውነት ማለት

9

How We Are

I call my brother.
"Yes," he answers,
"How can I help?"

I call my sister.
"Yes" – see her running –
"Let me give you more."

Look how we are.
You, me, him, her, us:
All heroes to each other.

I remember
What's important now.

ከምኡ ኢ፡ና

ንሓወይ ጸዊዐዮ
ምሆይ! ኢሉኒ
እንታይ ኣሎ ዝዓዮ?

ንሓብተይ ጸዊዐያ
ኣቤት! ኢላትኒ
እንታይ ክውሰኽ ብጕ፡ያ?

በሉ ንሕናስ ከምኡ ኢ፡ና
ኣነ ንሸኻ ንሸኺ…ንሕና!
ንዓይ ንዳኻ ንዳኺ…ንዓና!
ዘኪረዮ ኣገዳሲ ኩ፡ይኑ ረኺበዮ

Poverty

I have nothing.
Have some! Taste!
If we share,
We can bear
The worst poverty,
And it will pass.
Yet if we see

Others in need
And run away,
Forgetting even to say
"God bless. Good day"
Our poverty
Has only been replaced
By greed.

ድኽነትሲ

ንቓደም በሉ! ወስ በሉ!
ጥዓሙ ልና! ካብ ዘይብልና

መን ከማና ተኻፈልና
ድኽነትሲ ንኽእላ ኢና
ክሳብ ዝሓልፈልና

ምስ ሓለፈልና ግን ንስስዕ ዶኾን?
ሓሊፉልናስ ንውግን ዶኾን ካብ ከማና?
ንርስዕ ዶኾን ጥዕና ይሃበልና?

Mirror

Dear Mirror,
Show us
What we know.
We're beautiful
As angels,

Not crooked,
And beady eyed
With flat, runny noses,
Bad teeth,
Fat lips
And huge jaws
Hung like beaks
On giant heads
With big ears
And bad hair –
Messy and too long
Or barely there,
Though never bald.

Reflect
Anything imperfect
And we bust your glass.

መስትያት

መስትያት
እሰከ ርኣይና
ጽቡቃት እንዲና
ጽቡቃት በልና

መላእኽቲ ንመስል
ቴናን / ሜናን
ጨምጫም / ቄላዕ
ነፋጥ / ዓፋፍ / ጠፍናኞ
ሸራፍ / ጐራፍ / ጀላዕ
ሞጥማጥ / መንጋግ / ነግናግ
ኣዛን / ዘጋፍ / ወንጫር
በራሕ / መላጥ / ርእሲ ብሊቃ
የብልናን!

እንከን ከይተውጽእልና
ስብርብር ከነብለኪ ኢና ስብርብር!

15

Love Weather

Inviting
Wide eyes
Like lightning
Lift my heart

Sugar
Honey
And soul
For breakfast
Lunch
And dinner
Prime my heart

Uh-oh
Busted
Deserted
And waking up
To a nightmare
Burn my heart

Tomorrow
Or the next day
Wide eyes
May begin
Inviting again

እዋናት ፍቕሪ

እምባሕ!
ቂሕ!
ማሕ!
ልበይ ባሀ...

ሸኮር!
ምዓር!
ነፍሲ!
ምሳሕ!
ድራር!
ቁርሲ!
ልበይ ስራሕ...

ብህርር!
ብርር!
ዕግርግር!
ዕዝር!
ልበይ ሕርር...

ጽባሕ
ድሕሪ ጽባሕ
እንደገና እምባሕ!
ምናልባት...

17

Love in the Daytime

My lover
Shines like the sun.
I may be burned
Black as a frying pan,
Sweating buckets
And keeling over
With vertigo,
But why worry?

My lover
Shines like the sun.
She pours over my body
And breathes into my soul.
It feels so good
When she lights
My love on fire
Like dry wood.

ፍቕሪ ብቛትሪ

ጽሓየይ ንሳ
እንተጸለምኩ
እንተመሰልኩ ሞቝሎ
እንተርሃጽኩ
ርሃጽ ብሰንኬሎ
ብኮልጋ ዲ ሶለ
ሰንከልከል ኢለ
እንተቝረብኩ ክዕሎ
ብኣይ ኣይትሰከፉ
ከምኡ ዝገብር ፍቕሪ ኣሎ

ጽሓየይ ንሳ
ስጋይ ዳህሲሳ ነፍሰይ ቀስቂሳ
ሓዊ ኣጒዳትለይ ፍቕረይ ኣናኺሳ

19

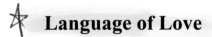

Language of Love

She said, "Flattery
Will get you nowhere,
Though you can try."

With my praise
Came pleasure,
Though she said, "You lie."

Love should use poetry.
She showed me why.

ምሂራትኒ ፎቘርኛ

እንተኾነ
ዝንኣድ የብለይኒ
ግዳስ
ባህ ክብለኒ
አፍካ አይትኽፈት
ብዘይካ ክትንእደኒ ኢላትኒ

ንኢደያ
ባህ ኢሉዋ
ሓሳዊ ኢላትኒ

ምሂራትኒ ፎቘርኛ
ሓውሲ ትግርኛ

Love Riddle

Touching me, her words
Said, "Mine."

She couldn't see
Or hear me.
I had no smell or taste.
Her hands felt nothing.

How many senses
Does this woman have?

ህዋሳታ

በዒንታ አይርአየትንን
በእዛና አይሰምዓትንን
ብኣፍንጭኣ አይሸተተትንን
ብመልሓሳ አይጥዓመትንን
በእዳዋ አይተንከፈትንን

ዝተንከፈትኒ ብቻላታ
ዝገበረትኒ ናታ
እዛ ሓብተይ ክንደይ ድየን ህዋሳታ?

23

"I love you"

"I love you, I love you" –
I thought I let it show.
Was that an "I love you, too"
In her glance?
I had to know.

"Let's dance!"
I beat the drum
And clapped the beat.
I was in heat –
Ezm-z-ezm! Ezm-z-ezm! –
Dancing with myself.

Passion as my witness,
Standing as charged,
Mounting my own defense,
As judge and jury no less,
I embraced my sentence.

She never looked, not even once.

አፍቅረኪ ኢለያ

አፍቅረኪ ኢለያ ተበሪሁኒ
አፍቅረካስ አይበለትንን
ከምኡ ድኣ ተሰሚዑኒ
ናይ ፍቅራስ ያኢ ባዕለይ ወሳኒ

ባዕለይ ከበሮ
ባዕለይ ጣቕዒት
ባዕለይ ጓይላ
ባዕለይ ሳዕስዒት
እዝም-ዝ-እዝም!

እወሓስ ባዕለይ አይትሓዙኒ
አግብእ ባዕለይ ምስክረይ ወኒ
ቀኁሊሕከ ቀኁሊሕ እንተተብለኒ
ብያነይ ባዕለይ በያኒ

25

"I love you" II

Young and afraid
I should have said
"I love you."

I hear her reply:
"You really want me? Ssshh.
Send your father to mine."

Shy, greener than green,
I couldn't say it.
"I love you."

እንተዝብላ

ደፊረ እንተዝብላ ኔረ
አንቲ ሓብተይ ነዓኺ አፍቂረ
እንታይ ኮን ምበለት?

ሱ፞ቅ በል በጃኻ
ቁምነገር እንተደሊኻ
ናብ አቦይ ዘይትሰዶ ነቦኻ?

አፍቂረያስ ኔረ
አይበልኩዋን ሓፊረ
አንታ ሸዉስ ጥረ እየ ኔረ ጥረ!

27

Ferenji (Frenchy) and Habesha

Hey sugar.
Hey shkor.
Come 'ere honey.
I love you, mAr.
Oooh, my sweetest.
You're the best.
I'm crispy little bread.
I'm hard thick crust.
Have some honey wine.
Taste this dark sorghum beer.
Do we need a car?
Nah, a mule suits us fine.
Let's build a home.
We'll make it like our poem.
Near the city for fun.
But far enough away to relax in.
Hey Habbash. What you want Frenchy?
Kiss me. Not in public, sweet ass.

I will call you ፈረንጂ

You say sugar
I say ሽኮር
You say honey
I say ምዓር
You are sweeter by far!

ስምዕኒ እምብኣር
We will eat ቅጫ
We will eat ጎጎ
We will eat ሕምባሻ
We will drink ሜስ
And ሱዋ ዳጉሳ
We will buy a በ፝ቆሊ
For our መገሻ
We will build a ህድሞ
In ዓዲ ሓውሻ

I will call you ፈረንጂ
You can call me ሓበሻ
I don't kiss in public: that is like ዓሻ!

29

Whose Daughter?

If I can't have her
Every morning everyday
My head aches.

I take her at breakfast
And after breakfast.
I want her at lunch
And after lunch.
I need her at dinner
And after dinner.

She slides through my lips
And licks my tongue.
She comes in my mouth
And I'm a man
Down to my core.

Burning incense,
I take her leisurely
On my sheepskin at home.
If I need her really bad,
Any bar we're in will do,
And I take her standing up.

ጓል መን እያ?

ወግሐ ጸብሐ
እንተዘይረኸብኩዋ
ርእሰይ እሓምም

ግዜ ቖርሲ
ግዜ ቖርስን ፈረቓን
ግዜ ምሳሕ
ግዜ ምሳሕን ፈረቓን
ግዜ ድራር
ግዜ ድራርን ፈረቓን
ምስኣ ኣለኹ ጥቓን ጥቓን

ብኸናፍረይ ትሰሉኽ
መልሓሰይ ልሕስ
ልበይ ትርክስ
ነፍሰይ ምልስ

ሓንሳእ ሓንሳእ ብወግዒ
ኣጎዛ ኣንጺፍና ኣብ ገዛና
ዕጣን ቡን እናበልና
ሓንሳእ ሓንሳእ ብደውና
ኣብ ባንኮ ተጸጊዕና
ንራኸብ ጥራይ ዝገበርና ጌርና

31

Whose daughter would do this,
Kiss after kiss after kiss
All day and all nightlong?
Is such behavior wrong?
Look in your pot on the fire.
I'll tell you her name – coffee.

እዚ ሰብአይ ተሃኒኑ
ኣይርኢ ዓይኑ ኣይሰምዕ እዝኑ
ጓል መንያ ትብሉ ቸኹኑ
ቀስቂሳቶ እምብዛ / ቀስቂሳቶ ወኑ
ጓል ጀበና እያ በሉ / ጓል ጀበና / ቡኑ

33

Talking about Love

Talking about love
Depends…
Is it hot or cold?

Talking about love
Doesn't end.
Is it sour or sweet?

Talking about love,
Don't pretend.
The human heart

Gave birth to love
And an identical twin –
Hate –

Stalking us to this day.
Talking about love
We deal with both.

ብዛዕባ ፍቕሪ

ብዛዕባ ፍቕሪ
ክንዛረብ ከሎና
ንገሊኦም ማሙቝ
ንገሊኦም ቀኈሪ
ምኽኒ ይገርመና

ብዛዕባ ፍቕሪ
ክንዛረብ ከሎና
ንገሊኦም ዕሪ
ንገሊኦም ምዓር
ምኽኒ ይገርመና

ብዛዕባ ፍቕሪ
ክንዛረብ ከሎና
ጽልኢ ኣላ ትጸናጸነና
ኢሂ ድአ ኣንተበልና ክበርሃልና
ፍቕርን ጽልእን እሕዋት እየን
ልብና እያ ወላዲተን ኣዲአን
ምናን ክናን ማናቱ እየን

35

Team or Twins

Left – right
Black – white
Open – bite
Peace – fight
Stop.
What is this?
Team or twins?
Twins or team?
Don't confuse the seam
With how to win.

ማንታ ወይ ጋንታ

ጋም-ማን!
ጸሊም-ጸዕዳ!
ጋም-ማን! ጋም-ማን!
ጸሊም-ጸዕዳ! ጸሊም-ጸዕዳ!
ደው በል!

ማንታ ድዮም?
እንድዕሎም ገሊአም ማንታ ይብሉዎም
ገሊአም ጋንታ አይፈላለዩን እዮም

Incompatible

A cat sings to a mouse,
And it sings back the same,
Which a dog barks to the cat,
Who doesn't change its tune.

Fire and straw join in.
Neither changes a note.
Now let the eyes and mote
Complete the refrain.

"My one and only,
Marry me.
I'm strong.
Can't we just get along?"

They're playing our song.

ደልየኪ ኔሪ

ደልየኪ ኔሪ
ኣነስ ንለይ ንሓዳሪ
ኣነስ ንለይ ንቌምነገሪ
እንታይ እሞ ይገብሪ
ባህርና እንድዩ ዘይሰመሪ

ድሙ ነንጭኳዋ
ኣንጭኳዋ ንድሙ
ድሙ ንኽልቢ
ክልቢ ንድሙ
ሓሰር ንሓዊ
ሓዊ ንሓሰር
በሰር ንዓይኒ
ዓይኒ ንበሰር

ደልየኪ ኔሪ
ኣነስ ንለይ ንሓዳሪ
ኣነስ ንለይ ንቌምነገሪ
እንታይ እሞ ይገብሪ
ባህርና እንድዩ ዘይሰመሪ

A Mother's Prayer

Bless this daughter in my arms
And bless this dream in my heart
Of eating porridge with butter
When she's grown up and married
And her children call me grandma.

Bless this son in my arms
And bless this dream in my heart
Of eating porridge with butter
When he's grown up and married
And his children call me grandma.

Bless me and Godspeed.
Let them blossom and be married,
Growing into a village
Of their own and making it warm.

ጸሎት ብዓል ኣደይ

ኣብ ኢ.ደይ ቄልዓ
ኣብ ልበይ ሕልሚ
ግዓት ክበልዕ
ግዓት ጠስሚ
ጓለይ ዓብያ
ተመርዕያ
ክትወልደለይ
ኣደዓባይ ዝብሉኒ

ኣብ ኢ.ደይ ቄልዓ
ኣብ ልበይ ሕልሚ
ግዓት ክበልዕ
ግዓት ጠስሚ
ወደይ ዓብዩ
ተመርዕዩ
ክወልደለይ
ኣደዓባይ ዝብሉኒ

መርቝኒ ይመልኣለይ
መርቝኒ የዕብየለይ
ከምስሉም ባዕለይ
ክፈርዩለይ
ዓዲ ክኾኑ ከማሙቝኑለይ

41

"Take a Walk on Sunday"

Sunday, Sunday
Take a walk on Sunday

No more being carried 'round
No more locked inside
No more crawling like a mouse
I'm going to hit my stride

Sunday, Sunday
Take a walk on Sunday

Mommy says, "Hey you, slow down"
Watch me run right past her
So what if I fall on my face
I'll get up and go faster

Sunday, Sunday
Take a walk on Sunday

ታተ! ታተ! ታተ!

ታተ! ታተ! ታተ!
እግሪ ሃብኒ ሰምበተ!

ዝኣኽለኒ ዓዲ ውዒለ
ዝኣኽለኒ ተሓዚለ
ዝኣኽለኒ ፍሑኽ ኢለ
ሕጂስ ኸኸይድ እግሪ ተኺለ
ክጉዪ! ክዘልል! ክነጥር! ክድብለ!

ታተ! ታተ! ታተ!
እግሪ ሃብኒ ሰምበተ!

ቀስ በል ኣታ ወደይ
ከይትወድቕ ትብለኒ ኣደይ
እንተወደቕኩ እንታይ ግደይ
እትስእ እነግፍ ሓመደይ
እስጉም እቕጽል መገደይ

ታተ! ታተ! ታተ!
እግሪ ሃብኒ ሰምበተ!

43

I'll cross rivers and mountains
That you would never dare
I'll ask the world why some are blessed
And others go nowhere

Sunday, Sunday
Take a walk on Sunday

ክሰግራ እየ እዛ ሩባ
ክተግራ እየ እዛ ኹርባ
ንዓለም ከዛርባ
እንታይ እዩ ሰበባ
ንገለን ራህዋ ንገለን ጸበባ

ታተ! ታተ! ታተ!
እግሪ ሃብኒ ሰምበተ!

They Raised Us

In the days of no telephones
And no writing letters,
We kids delivered the messages,
Beginning "My...my...my Mom."

I remember my mother saying,
"Come here, my angel, my son,
Go ask...." I remember
The mothers' names: Abrehet, light,

Mhret, forgiveness, Mahliet, song.
"My...my...my sweet Mom wants to know,
Please, if she can borrow some fire...
Sugar...coffee...salt...berbere?"

Yet we would run through the village,
Begin "My...my...my" and pause,
Out of breath and forgetting the message
Until we were offered bread.

ዘዕበያና

ስልኪ ዘይትድውልልላ
ወረቓት ዘይትጽሕፍላ
ከይተባህለት ከላ
ኣደይሲ! ኣደይሲ! እናበልና
ክንደይ መልእኽቲ ኣብጺሕና ኢና

ንዓ ዝወደይ መልኣኽ
ናብ ኣዴኻ ኣብርሀት
ናብ ኣዴኻ ምሕረት
ናብ ኣዴኻ ማህሌት ተልኣኽ

ሓዊ ዝንሃረ ሽኮር ዝመቀረ
ቡን ዝመረረ ጨው በረበረ
ሓርጭ ጥረ-ምረ
ኣለቅሕኒ ኢላትኪ ኣደይ ምዓረ

ጉያ ጉያ ኬድና
ካብኡ ናብኡ ኣብ ከብዲ ዓድና
ኣደይሲ! ኣደይሲ! ንብል ላህሊህና
እንተዘይሃባና ነፍ መልእኽትና ንርስዕ ኣብ ሞንጎ

47

We accepted, though not from everyone,
As Mom warned: even hungry angels
Sometimes had to say, "No thanks."
But forget being angels on the days

We'd hide behind our houses and pretend
Not to hear her call and call and call.
"Devils, just you wait until your father
Comes home. You'll be punished."

They called us angels and devils
And they raised us either way.

ኔረን ዝህባና
ከይንቅበል ሱቐ ኢልና
(መላእኽቲ እንዲና)
ጸጊብና ንብል ከይጸገብና
ከምኡ በል ተባሂልና በዴታትና

መዓልቲ ኔሩና
ተሓባእ ዝመጸና
ሸርብ ድሕሪ ገዛና
አጽቅጥ ከምዘይሰማዕና
ጋኔን ክብላና ክንቅጻዕ
ጽናሕ እሞ አቦኻ ይምጻእ

ዝልአኽ መልአኽ! ዘይልአኽ ጋኔን!
ዘዕበያና ከምዚ ኢለን እየን

Before the Birth of Toys

Near the cattle pen
In front of my parents' house
I found an empty olive oil can.
Who would throw it there?
No one I knew ate so well.

I took a knife from the kitchen
And cut four holes in the tin.
I made the wheels from clay,
Beat fleshy jute leaves into string
And carefully tied it to the thing.

Vrrooom. Vrroom. Vrrrooomm.
What a great truck to pull around!
I built it a road out of sand
Painted black with powdered dung.
My sister came and I warned her,

"Don't you touch my truck or dare
Cross my highway," but she said
"C'mon. Let me take your car
For a spin, and I'll teach you how to play
Handa with pebbles" – a sissy game for boys,

Before the birth of toys.

ባምቡላ ከይተወልዳ

እንዳ ዓለቦይ
አብቲ ጥቓ ደምበ
ታኒካ አልዮ አሊ፞ ረኺበ
መን ኮን ይኸውን ዝሰንደዋ ምስ ጸገበ

አብ ውሻጠ ካራ ረኺበ
ታኒካይ አንኩላ አርሒበ
ጭቃ ጠፍጢፈ አኽቢበ
መንኩርኩር ሰሪሐ አላጊበ
ኂቃ አልፈ0 ፍሒስ ገመደይ ቀሪበ
ቂጺረ ጐቲተ ስሒበ
ማኪናይ ሰሪሐየ ተጣቢበ
ካሚዮንጪኖ ናይ ሑጻ

ሹም! ሹም! አቢለያ ዘዊረያ
ባዕለይ ሰሪሐላ ጥውይውይ ጽርግያ
አጸሊመዮ ለኽየዮ ቦያ
ነስ አቢለሉ ንቑጽ ፋንድያ
ንሓብተይ ኢለያ አጠንቂቖያ
ከይትሰግርያ ከይትረግጽያ

ሓብተይ ኢላትኒ ንዓ እንዶ ግዳ
መኪናኻ ሓንሳእ ከኾብድዳ
ከርእየካ እየ ድሓር አጸውታ ሓንዳ
ከምዚሎ᎑ ባምቡላ ከይተወልዳ

51

Mother Courage

We have plenty of water
And we carry it to her
But Mother Courage,
Making porridge
With her tears,

Says "Here.
My children
Must be worthy,
Brave and strong
When we face trouble.
Eat."

ኣደይ ጽንዓት

ኣደይ ጽንዓት
ግዒታትለይ ግዓት...ብንብዓት!

ኣይውሓዳን ማይ
ኣይውሓዳን ወራድ ማይ
ከምዚ ኸማይ

ግዳስ...ኣብ ግዜ ምዓት
ክነፍዓላ ከምቶም ንፉዓት
ክብርትዓላ ከምቶም ብርቱዓት
ክበኸዓላ ከምቶም ብቑዓት...ደቃ

"Be a Man"

Don't say
"Be a man."
I was born this way
And do what I can.

"Be human.
Find a woman"
Sounds better to me.
May I be worthy

Of the woman
Who agrees
And makes me
Her man.

ሰብአይ ኩን!

ሰብአይ ተፈጢረ
ሰብአይ ኩን ንዝብለኒ
ሰብአይ ድአ ዕድለይ እንድዩ
አበይ ከይከደኒ?

ሰብአይ ኩን ዝበለኒ
አይመኸረንን!

ዝመኸረኒ
ሰበይቲ አምጽእ
ሰብ ኩን ዝበለኒ

አይ ሰበይቲ እንድያ
ሰብ ትገብር ንሰብአይ!

55

And Now?

Where's the "I love you, hmmmmm…
A bed of acacia thorns
Would be sweet with you"
From before the wedding?

The years and children
Take their toll.
"Ahhhhh!" you seem to announce,
Coming to bed now –

"Ahhhhh…Ahhhhh!"
In case she's thinking
"Let's make…" before
You "Kukkkkkkkk….Snorhhhhhhh."

ሕጂ ድኣ...

ቅድሚ መርዓ
ምሳኽስ ኣብ እሾኽ!
ምሳኽስ ኣብ ጭዓ!

ድሕሪ መርዓ
ሓደ ጨልዓ
ክልተ ጨልዓ
ጨልዓ ብጨልዓ
ደፋጫእ በሊዓ

ሕጂ ድኣ...
ድሓር ክኣስ...
እናበልካስ...ድቃስ...
ኩኽኽኽኽኽኽኽኽኽኽ!

Where Were You?

Shshshshshshshshsh!
The kids are sleeping.
Lower your voice
Or they'll be up.
Of course they ate.
They missed their daddy
And wanted to play.
"Where's my bedtime story?
Will we be alright?"
Where were you?

ኣበይ ኔርካ?

ሽሽሽሽሽሽሽሽ!
ቀስ በል ዘርኣም
ደቂሶም ኣለዉ እቶም ቤልዑ
ከይተበራብሮም

ተደሪሮም?

ምድራርስ ተደሪሮም
ደልዮም ኔሮም
ዝሕንግሮም
ዝጥብሮም ዝሕብሮም
ጽውጽዋይ ዝነግሮም
ኣጃኹም ዝበሎም
ደቀይ ሃብሮም
ኣበይ ኔርካ?

59

Women Have Time

Women have time
To breast feed,
Raise children
Clean house,
Wash, iron,
Fold clothes,
Carry water,
Gather wood,
Plant, weed, harvest,
Bake bread,
Make sauce,
Brew beer
And more:
Do their hair,
Kohl their eyes,
Add makeup,
Dress and undress.
Women have time
For a day at the office
And then to shop
For breakfast, lunch and dinner
That they prepare.

Women have time.
Men, we have no time.

ግዜ አለወን አንስትና!

ግዜ አለወን አንስትና
አጥቢያን/አዕቢያን
አጽርን/ገዛውትና
ሐጺበን/አስታሪረን
ዓጺፈን/ክዳውንትና
ማይ ወሪደን
ዕንጨይቲ ወፊረን
ጽህየን/ዓጺደን/እኽልና
ሰንኪተን/እንጌራና
ሰኽቲተን/ጸብሕና
ጸሚቘን/ሱዋና
ከይአኽለን/ገና
ተሓጺበን
ተጨኒነን
ተመሺጠን
ተኳሒለን
ተኽዲነን
አፈስ/ውዒለን/ምሳና
ገዚአን/አስቤዛና
ቀኑርስና! ምሳሕና! ድራርና!

ግዜ አለወን አንስትና!
ግዜ የብልናን ሰብኡት ኢና!

61

Sisters First

In the name of His mother, Mary,
You ask Jesus to listen
But abuse your own two sisters
Christened "Daughter of Mary"
And "Daughter of Christ."
You leave them with a curse,
As you're off to Mecca
And forgetting
What Jesus and Mohammed said:
Charity begins at home –
Sisters first.

በሕይወትካ ጀምር

ንብዓል ሚርያም
ንብዓል ለተማርያም
ርግጽ አቢልካ
በእንተ ማርያም ኢልካ
ናብ ክርስቶስ ስግር ክትብል ርእየካ
እሞ እንታይ በለካ?

በሕይወትካ ጀምር በሕይወትካ
አኽብረን ከኽብረካ ዶ ኢሉካ?

ምሓመድክ ከምኡ ዶ አይበለካን
መካ ምስ ክድካ?

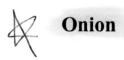 **Onion**

The wife peeled and cut an onion.
He had smacked her in the face.
Silenced, she prayed:

"Dear onion, please provide
An excuse for me to cry
So his mother won't say

'You deserved it!'
When she visits later today."
But the mother-in-law had sharp eyes.

"That onion may explain your tears
But not the black and blue.
Now what did you do?"

ሽጉርቲ

ጉንዲ እዝና ተጸፈዓ
ስና ኛኺሳ ነቢዓ
ይመጽ አሎዋ ሰሚዓ
ሕራይ ገበራ ከይብልአ
ሽጉርቲ ቀሪፋ ቀሊዓ
አመኽኒየለይ እስከ ንዓ

ሽጉርትስ የኸውን ነቲ ንብዓት
ይገድፍዶ ኢልኪዮ ስምብራት
ኢለንአ ይብሃል አደይ መብራት
አስተውዒለናላ ብዓይኒ ሓማት

65

Butter

Like butter
Left out in the sun
She melts to tears.
I want to help her
And find the guy
Who left her to die.
But she runs
Away from the shade

To cry in the hot sun.

ልኻይ

ልኻይ አብ ጽሓይ ክትበኪ ውዒላ
እንታይ ኮንኪ ኢለያ ሓዚነላ
ቴፍ በሊ ኢለያ ክዘርየላ

ልኻይ ተሓሲማ ንጽላላ
ተሓሳሚት ባዕላ ሸኻዩት ባዕላ
ንመን እሞ ንመን ክሃርመላ

ልኻይ አብ ጽሓይ ክትበኪ ውዒላ

"I Cut His Hair"

When he strutted down the street
Nobody could compete
With Samson and his hair.

Delilah, fresh out of beauty school,
Saw him and said, "You're cool."
She was beautiful and he proposed.

"Yes, oh yes, yes, yes," she cooed,
"And let me do your hair, it's great."
She made Samson into one handsome dude.

The wedding couldn't have been better.
Live music, poems, the best food and wine
And thousands of guests on the conga line

Cheering the newlyweds to their bed.
Lovely Delilah stripped, revealing her charms.
She welcomed Samson into her long arms

ወሪዱኒ ደላይላ!

ጸጉሩ ምስ አብቄሎ
ሳምሶን መን ክኽእሎ!
ሸዉ ትሓጸ
ብዓልቲ መላጸ...ደላይላ

ዘጋፍ ርእያቶ
ርእሱ ላጽያ
አጸበቖቶ

መርዓ ኾነ
ሰብ ተዓደመ
አውሎ ተባህለ
ማስ ተገጥመ
ምኣዲ ወርደ
ሱዋ ተሰትየ
ሜስ ተጠምጠመ
ዋሕስ ቄመ
መርዓ ተፈጸመ

ንቡር ክገብሩ
ንእዲ ምስ ተገሩ
ዕዮ ክይዓየየ

69

But he couldn't get it up and cried.
"She castrated him." His friends spread the word.
His mother screamed and shouted bloody murder.

Sad Delilah heard and calmly stared
Them in the eyes: "I didn't cut off his balls.
I cut his hair."

ጕሪድ ምስ ኣበየ
ሳምሶን ኣልቀሰ ሸኸየ
ኣዕሩኹ ጀመሩ ከማርሩ
ደላይላ እያ ከቶ ዝመከተቶ

ሓማት ደላይላ
ነዚኣ ሰሚዔን
ኣውያት ተኸላ

ወሪዱኒ ደላይላ!
ኣነ ዝጨረጽኩዎ ርእሱ
እንታይ ኣራኸቦ ምስ ፍረ ነብሱ?

"May We Live To See Your Wedding"

Remember the old blessing? –
"May we live to see your wedding."

It reminds me of a Chinese proverb:
We're cursed if our wishes come true,
And if they don't, we're cursed too.

Our children say
If we want to see them married
So much, they'll need
The wedding on video
And for us to pay.

Let them be implored
"May we live to hear your wedding"
And perhaps they'll want a radio.
This we could afford.

መርዳኹም የርእየና!

መርዳኹም የርእየና! ምርቓና
ምርኢይስ ርኢናዮ
ምስላ ቻይና ኩይኑና

ሃረረ ዝበልካዮ
እንተበጽሓካ ወዮ
እንተዘይበጽሓካ ወዮ

ክንርእዮ ካብ በልና ክንርእዮ
ይብሉ አለዉ ደቅና
አይንምርያን ብዘይ ቪድዮ!

መርዳኹም የስምዓና ዶ ኸንብል?
አይንምርያን ክብሉና ብዘይ ራድዮ!

Into Temptation

Married,
I love my bride
And we have a child.
I'm alone on a business trip

And wearing my watch
When I see her, temptation,
Moving towards me, her lips
Smiling to make me fall.

I smile back. Her "Hi"
Makes me quickly reply
"Hi," and "Sorry, I'm in a hurry,"
But she comes closer, saying

"Do you have the time?"
The time? I think. My watch.
"Do you have the time please?"
Yes, it's all she wants.
I tell her and she's gone.

I only tempt myself, true.
Sorry, girl, for laying this on you.

ባዕለይ ፈተና

ተመርዕየ እየ መርዓት ኣላትኒ
ወሊደ እየ ቤልዓ ኣላትኒ
ኣብዛ ቕልጽመይ ስዓት ኣላትኒ
ከተማ ከይደ ጉዳይ ኔራትኒ

ፈተና መጻት እናተገየጸት
ከተውድቖኒ ይመስለኒ

ፍሽኽ ኢላትኒ ፍሽኽ ኢለያ
ሰላም ኢላትኒ ሰላም ኢለያ
ድሕሪ ሰላም ተሃንጥየ ክብላ
ግዜ የብለይኒ!

ቅርብ ኢላ ዝበለትኒ
ስዓተይ ረሲዔያ ስዓት እንዶ ንገረኒ!

ንስዓት ዲኺ ስዓትሲ ኣላትኒ
ስዓት ነጊረያ ዕዝር ሓዲጋትኒ

ባዕለይ ፈተና ንባዕለይ
ኣሳጊበልኪ ሓብተይ ይቕረ በልለይ

75

Old Age

Our bodies and minds in old age
Depend on each other more
And work together less,
But we still turn the page.

Goodbye youth, innocence,
Jumping around sky high
And experience beyond belief –
Goodbye and thank you.

Thank God for the time to raise
And educate our children.
Thank God they've married and
Have children to brighten our days.

Housebound we still manage
Most of our daily needs
And know how to ask for the rest.
"Son, daughter, grandchild...."

Our words grow stronger everyday.
With a blessing or a curse,
We get our way.

እርጋን

እርጋን ከምኡ እዩ ዝገብር
ህዋሳት ምስ መሓውር
እስርስርስርስር!

ድሓን ኩኒ ጉብዝና
ክንድይ አኳ ርኢና
ክንደይ እኳ ዘሊልና
የቘንየልና

ዓዲ ውዒልና
ተመስገን ጐይታና
ዕድመ ዝሃብካና
ደቅና አዕቢና
ደቅና አምሂርና
ደቅና አመርዒና
ደቂ ደቅና ርኢና
ዝተረፈስ ነርክበሉ ብአፍና

ንዓ ተመረቕ ዝወደይ!
ንዒ ተመረጺ ዛንለይ!
አይአብዩናን ግዲ
ክረግመኪ እየ አቲ ጨልዓ!
ክረግመካ እየ አታ ወዲ!
አለና እኮ መገደዲ

Our bodies and minds in old age
Depend on each other more
And work together less,
But we still turn the page.

እርጋን ከምኡ እዩ ዝገብር
ህዋሳት ምስ መሓውር
እስርስርስርስርስር!

Old Timers

My father and mother
Gave me
What no one can take away.

My Land – Off.
House – Out.
Bed – Up.
This goatskin – Don't touch.
A legacy – Mine.

With all my education
And throughout my pursuits,
Have I added something new
Like salt and pepper
To an old stew?

Dear old timers,
If I ignore you
Or forget,
What am I? A sheep?
Baaaaaah?

ሰብ ቀደም

ናይ አቦይ ሓላለይ
ናይ አደይ ሓላለይ
መን እዩ ዝወስደለይ እስኪ!

ትንክፍ አዛ መሬት!
ትንክፍ አዛ ገዛ!
ትንክፍ እዛ ዓራት!
ትንክፍ እዛ አጎዛ!

ተማሂረ ተመራሚረ
እንታይ እየሞ ደሚረ
ንጨው ንበርበረ

ናይ ቀደም እንተ ረሲዐ
ሰብ ቀደም እንተ ዘንጊዐ
እሞ አነስ በጊዕ እየ
እምቤዕዕዕዕዕዕ!

My Rock

A huge sycamore
In Senafe
At the foot of Mount Meteora –
She grips a rock big as a house.
With St. Mary as her witness,
She loves him.

She's smart,
Remembering long ago:
When she ate bread
Not stone, the gift
She wrapped in her roots.
She still holds tight.

The ancient stone reveals
That the mystery of what has been
Will change to bread again.

ደንጉላይ

ዓዳ ሰንዓፈ
ገዘውታ እግሪ መጠራ
ኪዳነ ምህረት ትመስክር
ምስ ከውሒ ተፋቒራ
ሕቖፍቀኖፍ ተጠማሚራ
ንዳዕሮዱ ክብላ ዶንቀኖራ

ብዘበን ኢኔ ኢኔ
ሕምባሻ ከሎ እምኒ
ህብስተይ ኢላ ንዕድኖላ
በመጽዓን ሰራዉራ
ከረው አቢላ ጠቘሊላ
ዝሓቜፈቶ ደንጉላ
ሕጇ ውን ሓቖኑፉቶላ
እንታይ ድዩ ምስጢሩ
ሕምባሻ እንተኾይኑ
መዋእሉ ቄጺሩ
አብ ሕምባሻ ምʼቒያሩ
አይተርፎንዩ

Impossible
Or just too slowly for you?
Then let the rock stay –
Smart Sycamore,
My rock.

እንተዘይተቓይሩ
ይጽናሕ ተጠሚሩ!

ዳዕሮዶ ሃላይ?
ደንጉላይዮ ደንጉላይ
ብደንጉልኡ እንተላይ!

Old Sayings

Think about doing the right thing
And the words
"There is an old saying..."
Offer a little wisdom
That's been forgotten
Or lost in some elder's head.

An old crow says to his son,
"We crows have a saying:
Trust a man until he bends
To pick up a stone."

But the young crow answers back.
"Why wait until he bends?
What if the man has a rock
In his pocket?"

Stumped, the old crow caws,
"I've never heard such notions.
What is the world coming to?"

ባህሊ ናይ ትማሊ

ካብቲ ቀደም ዝተባህለ
ዝእክቦ ስኢኑ ኮረር ዝበለ
እሞ ዝተረስዐ ምስ ጐደለ
ዘኪረዮ ዝብል እንተለ
ብሁል ይብሃል ባህሊ ዝተባህለ

ባህሊ ናይ ትማሊ ይምከርኩም
ግዜ ኽኣ ይንገርኩም

ንኣብነት ኸኹነኩም
ናይ ኲኽ ከምጽኣልኩም
ኲኽ ንወዱ መኺረ ክብል በለ
እምኒ ከልዕል ድንን እንተዘይበለ
ሰብ ኣይትፍራህ ዝወደይ ጨለ

ወዲ ኲኽ ወዲ ዘቡ
ነቡኡ ሓተቶ ለባም ኮይኑ
ብዓል ኣቦይ ንሰብ ትኣምኑ
እምኒ ክሳብ ዘልዕል ደኒኑ
እንተመጸኸ መኺሩ ኣሊኑ
ኣብ ጀቡኡ ሓቢኡ እምኑ

ኣቦ ኲኽ ገሪሙዎ
ኣነስ በልኩኻ ቀዳሞት ዝበሉዎ
እዚ ኸፍኣት ግዜኻ ኣምጺኡዎ
ህይ...ባህሊ እውን ለካ ግዜ ኣለዎ!

87

Do Unto Others?

She knows today
She's right
Not to stand
By all her elders say.

Consider
"Love those who love you.
Hate those who hate you, too."

Her enemies delight
In loving to hate her and
Hating to love her.

እንተትመኽራ

ትማሲ ንሎሚ እንተትመኽራ
ጸላኢኺ ጽልኢ ፈታዊኺ ፍተዊ
ምበለታ ኔራ

ምዕባየይ ኢላ ምሰምዓታ
ምኽኖነት ክኣ መፍቶ ጸላእታ
ክጸልኡዋ ዝፈትዊዋታ
ክፈትዊዋ ዝጸልኡዋታ

Thread and Culture

Like people,
Like cloth;
Like culture
Like thread –

Sew or you're naked,
Commitment or you're dead.

Don't need culture?
Lose your thread?
You're crazy,
Cold and dead.

ፈትሊ ባህሊ

ዓለባ ይልገብ ብፈትሊ
ሰብ ይላገብ ብባህሊ
እቲ ኛኽዳን እቲ ኛኺዳን

ብዘይ ፈትሊ ዕርቃን
ብዘይ ባህሊ ዕብዳን

ባህሊ ምለኹ!
ፈትሊ ኣይትብተኹ!

The New Houses

I think of the hot pan
We use for cooking bread –
The metal not the clay –
When I see the tin roof
On shiny new houses.

A lot of us want them
Instead of the old places
Made of mud and wood.

How strange
That the new houses use
The same water from the sky
And fire from the sun
But fry us children

Of Adam and Eve.
In our old mud houses
We used to come out red.
If we descended from
Corn and sorghum

We would pop
In our shiny new houses
And come out white.

መረባዕ

እቲ መረባዕ
ሞቝሎ ክብለኺ ይግባእ

እወ ሞቝሎ ምሓዛ ሞነነ
መሰንከት ቅጭ መሰንከት ነነ

ህድሞና አሪጉ በልዩ
ብዙሓት እዮም ንዳኺ ዝደልዩ

ናትክስ ጉዳም
ማይኪ ካብ ሰማይ
ሓውኺ ካብ ጸሓይ
እቲ እትስንክትዮ እትጨልውዮ
አብ ውሽጣኺ ዘሎ ሓሳኺ
ወዲ አዳም ከምዚ ኸማይ

ቀያሕቲ ኔርና አብታ ህድሞና
ሎምስ ኬድና ጸሊምና

ከይንጽዕዱ ተጨሊና
ካብ ዕፉንዶ ካብ መሻላ ተወሊድና ኢልክና

93

A Saying

A saying contains more
Than what has been said before.
Who says what now,
To whom and how?
How does the saying sound?
What about the background
Of the saying? Who is the person
Who remembers it and recites?
On what occasion?
Who read the saying? Where?
Who wrote it down to share?
A saying means discussion,
ABCs and learning to read and write.

ባህሊ

መን በሃሊ
እንታይ በሃሊ
ንመን በሃሊ
በየናይ መበሃሃሊ
እንክንብል ባህሊ
ወ ዉ ዊ ዋ ዌ ው ዎ
መን ዘኪሩዎ? መን ደጊሙዎ?
መን ጽሒፉዎ? መን አንቢብዎ?
ሃ ሁ ተመሃሩ
ፈ ፉ ጽሓፉ
በ ቡ አንብቡ

The Book of My Ancestors

We go to work
To pay for our daily bread.
But with the land
I inherited
And education for my tool
I have a question:
How do I live?

Are there any answers
Besides hearsay,
The Holy Book
And the same old advice?-

You know what's right.
You've heard the truth
And been given
The chapter and verse.
If you want more,
Take a vacation down the shore.
Maybe the fish will bite.

አበይ አሎ መጽሐፍ አቦታተይ?

ንመግቢ ዕለተይ
ምስ አሕዋተይ
ሃሰስ ናተይ

ርስተይ መሬተይ
ሓኽለይ ትምህርተይ
እንታይ ግበር ትብሉኒ
አበይ አሎ መጽሓፍ አቦታተይ?

አታ ወደይ አይትብል ሓፍሓፍ
ናይ መሬት ብአፍ
ናይ ሰማይ ብመጽሓፍ
ክንድዚ ህልቀኑ ክንድዚ ምዕራፍ
ብዝተረፈ ባሕሪ ኼድካ ዓሳ ምግፋፍ

White Paper

Take
White paper,
Ink, and writing
Like black fruit –

White with a lot
Of black, I mean
A lot of black
On white –

Open wide,
And the whole world
Wakes up.

Take paper
Without the black,
The spine
And the inky fruit
And you can wrap
Sugar and coffee.

ጸዕዳ ወረቐት

ጸዕዳ ወረቐት
ጸሊም እያ ትፈሪ

ጸሊም ጽሕፈት
ጸሊም ቀለም
ጸሊም ሕብሪ
ንምሉእ ዓለም
መበራብሪ መሸረፈት

ጸዕዳ ወረቐት
ወይዛ ሕልፈት
ጸሊም ገደፈት
መጠቕለል ቡን
መጠቕለል ሽኮር
ኮይና ምተረፈት

Literature

Alphabets
Make words.

Words make
Statements.

Statements join
Literature.

Literature invites
The world: Be like me.
The world looks
And says
You still need to cook
But I'll marry you someday.

Sssssssss bubble
Bubblebub Rrrooohhhllling
Simmer simmer simmer

ቀለም

ፊደላት
መሰረት ቃላት

ቃላት
መሰረት ባህላት

ባህላት
መሰረት አባላት ቀለም

ቀለም ንዓለም
ንዓይ ምሰሊ!
ዓለም ንቋለም
ቅድም ብሰሊ!
ዕሰሊየ ክብለልኪ ዕሰሊ!

ፍሮቘሮቘ! ፌሮቘሮቘ!
ፌሮቘሮቘ! ፌሮቘሮቘ!
ፌሮቘሮቘ! ፌሮቘሮቘ!

The Letters Get Drunk

Let's get drunk tonight,
The letters say.
When C, A, and T
Start meowing
And D, O, and G
Start bow-wowing
It's love at first sight.
Meow. Meow!
Bow-wow. Bow-wow!
Meow! Bow-wow!
Till dawn the next day.

A real dog and cat –
Who normally, in the fur,
Relate like fire and water,
Eyes and dust –
See the letters
Look like them and kiss.
What to do?
For once the cat and dog agree:
"We have a reputation to restore."
They go back to scratching and biting
Each other, worse than before.

ፈደላት ሸኺሮም

ፈደላት ሸኺሮም
ድን ሙን
ኛው! ክብሉ ጀሚሮም
ከን ልን ቢን
ዊሕ! ክብሉ ጀሚሮም
ሸዑ ንሸዑ ተፋቒሮም
ኛው-ኛው! ዊሕ-ዊሕ!
ኛው-ኛው! ዊሕ-ዊሕ!
ክሳብ ትወግሕ!

ድሙን ከልብን
እቶም አርባዐተ እግሮም
ወወሰኖም ሒዞም
ይዕዘቡ ኔሮም

ድሙን ከልብን
ሓውን ሓሰርን
ዓይንን ሓመድን
ካብ መፈጠሮም
እዞም ፈደላት ዘይሕዙ ሰፈሮም
ሎምስ ከአ ከብሉና ተፋቒሮም?
እናበሉ
ሸዑ ንሸዑ ተፈሓጢሮም
መሓለው ክብሮም

103

Words

In the beginning
The mouth and tongue
In harmony said
Let there be words
Stored in our head,
Marked on sheepskins,
Sown by books,
Scattered by newspapers,
Broadcast by radios,
Diffused by TVs,
Spread and overspread
With telecommunications
And the internet
To connect or disconnect us
Wherever we are –
Near or far,
In the present or past –
To reconnect one world
As never before.
The mouth and tongue
Gave us this gift of God.
Anyone who forbids words
Or forbids us to use them
Better reckon with him
Before trying to take away
Our trusty tool.

ቃል

ኣብ መጀመርያ ዝነበረ
ምስ ኣፍ ምስ መልሓስ ዝሓበረ
ኣብ ርእሲ ኣብ ብራና
ዝሓደረ! ዝሰፈረ!
ብጋዜጣ ብመጽሓፍ ዝተናጠረ
ብራድዮ ብተለቪዥን ዝተወርወረ
ብተለ መለ ብኢንተርነት ዝተዘርዘረ
ንዝሓለፈ ምስ ዘሎ ዝኣሳሰረ
ንርሑቕ ኣብ ቀረባ ዘንበረ
ሓድነት ደቂ ኤረ
ኣብ ዘለዉዎ ሃገረ
ዘህጠረ ዝዕበረ
ቃል ይብሃል
ህያብ እግዚኣቢሄር ዝኸበረ

ሱቕ በሉ ዝብለና
ከም ንብል ዝገብረና
ከይወጽእ ቃልና
ይኽልኣልና! ቃልዩ ሓኸልና!

105

One Word, Two…

I take one word,
Then two, rub them and…
Hey, look! Fire!

Women, stay home.
Gather no more wood.
My words will do.
I'll give them to you.

Please, enough fuss.
We've told you before.
You call this fire?
Wuss.

ቃልቃል!

ቃል ንበይና ቃል
ምስ ካልኣይ ርእሳ
ቃልቃል!

ሓዊ ኣጕደ ሓዊ
ኣትን ኣንስቲ
ዝባን መንግስቲ
ከይትወፍራ ዕንጨይቲ!

ግዲ የብልካን!
ርእ,ናልካ ኣለና ሓወኻ!
እቶናይ ድኣ ከይብለኻ!

What & What Do You Call

Question said, "Dad.
You want me married
But why can't I choose?"

Whatever tried
To answer his son,
But everyone he found
Was too tall, too short,
Too thin, too fat,
Too red, too black.

"Alright," the father said,
"Already you're a problem.
Find your own bride."

Question struggled long
And hard to find
His one and only

But finally settled down.
She called him, "What,"
He named her "What do you call,"

And their son answered to "Why."

እንታይ? ክስታይ!

ሕቶ ኢሉዋ ነቡኡ
ካብ በልካስ አመርዕወኒ
ቅድም ግን አምርጸኒ

ዘምጽአሉ መልሲ
እዚኣስ ሓጺራ
እዚኣስ ነዊሓ
እዚኣስ ጠቂራ
እዚኣስ ቀሓ
እዚኣስ ዓቢራ
እዚኣስ ሰቢሓ
ኢሉዋሲ
በል ወደይሲ
ከይተምጽአለይ ባእሲ
ባዕልኻ ርኸብ መልሲ

ሓዲሩ ሓዲሩ
ብዙሕ ተሸጊሩ
ሕቶ ሓዳር ጌሩ

ንሱ እንታይ? ንሳ ክስታይ!
ወዲ ወሊዶም ተስታይ
ስለመንታይ? ሰምዮሞ ስለምንታይ?

109

To a Teacher

For God's sake,
Lose the stick today.
Nobody, young or old,
Learns language, science and math
That archaic, stupid way.
From our mountains to our seas
Each student deserves
What each teacher should expect:
Equality, dignity, respect,
Communicating peace
And every human right
For learning to burn bright.

ትምህርቲ ኣይኮነን!

ኣንታ ፈጣሪ
በዚ ሎሚ ምድሪ
ምኽሪ ገዲፍካስ በትሪ...ነውሪ!

ትምህርቲ ኣይኮነን
እንግሊዝ ቀኈጹሪ
ሳይንስ ኬምስትሪ

ትምህርቲ ኣይኮነን
ኤለመንታሪ
ፕራይመሪ
ሰኮንዳሪ

መምህራን ምድሪ ባሕሪ
እንተዘይሓሊና
ናይ ወዲ ሰብ ክብሪ
ብኣብነት ብግብሪ
ትምህርቲ ኣይኮነን!

The Raw, Hard Seed

These days, majority rules:
Cook every seed.
Let one, raw and hard,
Swear, "I like the way I am,"
And the majority demands,
"Be like us, you fool,"

Until a hungry man comes along:
"Cooked, uncooked, be damned."
He uses both hands,
Shoveling them all into his mouth.

Chew. Chew. Chew. Chew. Ow!
The raw, hard seed resists,
Breaking the man's tooth.

Disgusted he spits the seed out
And it promptly starts to root.

ጥረ እንታይ ገበረ?

ግዝአተ ብዙሓን ነበረ
ብዙሓት ዝበሰሉ
እንኮ ጥረ
ብሰልየ-ብሰል
ንዓና ምስል ዝተባህለ
ዘይሓበረ

ሰብ ከኣ መጸ
በሰለ አይበሰለ ከይመረጸ
ሕፍስ! ጉስም! ቀኑሕም!
ዝበሰለ ኹሉ ቅህም!

ጥረ እንታይ ገበረ?
ኮርምቲ ሰብ ሰበረ
ጡፍ ተባህለ ተባረረ
ኣብ መሬት ስፈረ
ክበቑል ጀመረ

The Smart Star

Seeing the star,
The sun said,
"You think you're so bright?
Out!"
And rose her lovely head.

The star went right to bed.
Smart.
She awoke at midnight
And the shepherds
Followed her light.

ጐሪሑ

ጽሓይ ንኮኸብ
ብርሃንካዶ ብርሃነይ ከሎ?
ትብል እሞ ትኽውሎ

ነዚኣ ፈሪሁ/ኮኸብ ጐሪሑ
ኣንጊሁ/ገስጊሱ/ኣንጊሁ
ጓሶት መሪሑ/ኣብ ጐይታና/ኣብጺሑ

After the Rain

Drip, splash, pour –
Sounds like rain
Falling down.
Pirrr, shhh, rruop –
Sounds like rain
Getting up?
No. Steam.

ውራይ ማይ

ማይ ካብ ሰማይ
ጥብ! ጥብ! ጥብ!

ማይ ንሰማይ
ጥር! ጥር! ፍንጥር!

ማይ ንሰማይ
ሓፍ! ሓፍ! ሃፉ!

Man and Button

A dark, rainy day
On the city limits
Where a man loses
His button,
Grabs a bus
To the market
And starts looking:

Can I help you?
I lost a button.
Where?
On the road.
Where?
At the city limits.
Why look here?

The light, the light, my son.

ብዓል መልጎም

መልጎም ጠፊኣቶ/ኣብ ጎዳይፍ
ጸልማት ኔሩ/ማይ ኪፍኪፍ
እቶቡስ ተሰዊሉ/ንሹ፞ቕ ኣቢሉ/ጽርግፍ!

ሹ፞ቕ ምስ በጽሐ
ኣብቲ ዝበርሀ
ሃሰወሰው...

መልጎም ጠፊኡኒ
ኣበይ?
ኣብ መገዲ
ኣበይ?
ጎዳይፍ ግዲ!
እንታይ ድኣ ኣብዚ ተናዲ?
እንተበርሃለይ ኣታ ወዲ!

119

Our Path

Waiting
On the straight
And narrow,
Squeezed tight
Between the taboos
Left and right,

And sitting still
Because the track
Has no way up
Ahead to jump
And nowhere to fall
Down or back,

Let's try
To be like trees,
Our roots and leaves
Reaching earth to sky.

መገድና

መገድና ቀጢና
ሓራም! ብጸጋማ
ነውሪ! ብየማና

ንቕድሚ ትከ? ጽናሕ!
ንድሕሪ ትከ? ኣይትበል!
ንላዕሊ ኸ? ኣይትዝለል!
ንታሕቲ ኸ? ኣይትንጠልጠል!

እሞ ኾፍ ንበል
ፍሕትሕት ኣይንበል
ሰራው ኢና ንበል
ሱር ንስደድ ንብቄል

Shoes

Tap tip tap tip
Clack clack click click
Op ip op ip
Scuff scuff scuff scuff
Swoosh swoosh swoosh swoosh
Creak creak creak creak
Whum whum whim whum
Squeak squeak squeak squeak
Uh-huh, uh-huh, uh-huh, uh-huh
Percuss, percuss, percuss, percuss

Wo-hhho. I'm on my back.
But I'm up and back on track.
Lousy shoes.

What an excuse!
Watch out where you're going.

ሳእነይ

ዓጨጭ! ዓጨጭ! ዓጨጭ!
ዓጠጥ! ዓጠጥ! ዓጠጥ!
ኩደብ! ኩደብ! ኩደብ!
ኒሕ! ኒሕ! ኒሕ!
ደርገፍ! ደርገፍ! ደርገፍ!
ሸለብ! ሸለብ! ሸለብ!
ጨፍለቅ! ጨፍለቅ! ጨፍለቅ!
ሸተት! ሓጠቅ! ብድድ!

እሂ ድአ ሳእነይ?
ከቢደኪ ድየ?

ወሪዱኒ ሳእንኻ!
ዘይትርኢ ዓይንኻ?

123

My Donkey Says

I put on my pants
One leg at a time
And my shoes one after the other.
What's to understand?

I see good and bad
And carry my stick in my hand.
Is peace ahead?
Is it a tough climb?

Listen. As my donkey says,
I've had many a day
Farting my way
Up cliffs like this.

እዛ ዓቐብ ከመይ?

እዛ ስረይ ቅድም ሓንቲ
ድሓር ካልአይቲ እግረይ

እዛ ሳእነይ ቅድም ሓንቲ
ድሓር ካልአይቲ እግረይ

ክፉእ ኣሎ ክፉእ
ጽቡቕ ኣሎ ጽቡቕ
በትረይ ኣብ ኢደይ በትረይ
ሰላም ንቕድመይ

እዛ ዓቐብ ከመይ?
ክንደይ ዓቐብ ዘይጠረጥኩ!
ትብል ኣድገይ

June 20

Remembering her martyrs
And child heroes,
She said to me today,
We suffer
To be Eritrean.

Many of us have died
To let the mighty know
We won't be conquered
And, though the rich have tried,
We won't be bought or sold.

Look at our children,
Made in the same mold.
Their mothers' prayers
To flower and bear fruit
Have been answered:

Children everywhere –
Strong, happy and free
Like lions and tigers.
When they see the hate
And envy in the eyes

Of the hunter and invader
The children say,
"Mother, please stay home.
Live in joy and peace.
We go to fight them."

ሰነ መበል ዕስራ

ሰነ መበል ዕስራ/ትብል ኤርትራ/ጀጋኑ ደቃ ዘኪራ

ዋዛ ኣይኮነን ኤርትራ ምኳን
ብርእሰኻ ምሕዳር ንርእሰኻ ምኳን

ብስም ሃብታማት ኣይገዝኡኻን
ብስም ሒያላት ኣይመልኩኻን
ደቕኻ ኣብ ቅድሜኻ
ኣሕሊፍም ኣይሀቡኻን...ኣባዳን!

ቃንዛ እዩ ወላዲት ምኳን
ትመባጸዕ ኣብ ፈጣሪ
ትዕምብብ ትፈሪ ተጥሪ
ገለ ኣምበሳ ገለ ነብሪ
ኣይስኣንን ዝቓንእ ዝኾኑሪ
ኸኸውን ዝብል ወራሪ ከታሪ
ኣደየ ይብሉኻ ይብገሱ ደቕኻ
ኣነ ኸኸይድ ንሽኺ ንበሪ!
ኣነ ኸኸይድ ንሽኺ ክበሪ!

127

Remembering her martyrs
And child heroes,
She said to me today,
We suffer
To be Eritrean.

ዋዛ አይኮነን ኤርትራ ምዃን
ብርእሰሽ ምሕዳር ንርእስሽ ምዃን

ሰነ መበል ዕስራ/ትብል ኤርትራ/ጀጋኑ ደቃ ዘኪራ

129

We Came Close

We came close to her – so close,
We thought she'd stay,
And you wouldn't take her away,
Though she belonged to you.

Why take her before us?
Our baby grew and went to school,
But we never saw her married.
Is our God jealous?

You called and she came,
Trailing all our tears.
Overflowing, they cried *Stay,*
Root yourself here,
Hoping to drown out your call.

What more can we say except
Parents, we can never have
Enough of our children and
Thanks to God we're not barren?

ካብኻዶ ቀሪበናያ?

ካብኻዶ ቀሪበናያ?
ዝወሰድካያ ናትካ እያ
መሲሉና ድኣ ኣይምሰልካ
ዘይተሓድግ እንኩ ምስ በልካ

ብኻ ቅድሚኣ ምወሰድካና
ወሊድና ኣዕቢና ኣምሂርና
መርዓኣ ከይተርእየና
ተቓጺጽካና ጐይታና ተቓጺጽካና

ከይዳ ኣላ ናብኻ ጸዊዕካያ
ኣዒንትና ኣኽቲላ እናበኸያ
ብርኽቲ ዘርኢ/መሬትኪ ርሒሳ/ጠልቅያ
ሱር ቶኽሊ/ኢለንእ/ኣብያ/ንሸኻ ትዓብያ

ምሳኻ ዝማጕት ኣፍ የብልናን
ወለድቲ ኢና ውላድና ኣይጸገብናን
ነመስግን ከአ ጸኒትና ኣይጸነትናን

131

Genet

Worldly-wise Genet
Did what she liked.
Asmara's Who's Who
Came to her funeral yesterday.

Genet was simply true.
She lived well.
She didn't ask.
She didn't tell.

Any of our regrets
That she's gone to her rest
Apply only to the desire
She's left deep in our breasts.

Asmara mourns the same.
But all her citizens in tears,
Genet won't reappear.
Let heaven have her today
Doing what she likes.

We won't forget her name
Until we also pass away.
We never had enough
Of dear Genet Tesfay.

ገነት ነበረት

አብዛ ዓለም ኔራ
ድላያ ጌራ
ትማሊ ተቐቢራ
አብ አስመራ

ገነት ነበረት
ገነት ገበረት
ኣይነገረት

ይዋእ ከይንብላ
ይዋእት ንሕና
ንሳስ ሓሊፋ
ሃረርታ ገዲፋ አብ ልብና

አስመራ ሸኽያ ምእንቲ ርእሳ
ሰብኣይ ሰበይቲ ንብዓታ አፍሲሳ
ኣይከኣለትን ንገነት ክትመልሳ
ገነት ከም ድላያ ንሳ
መንግስተ ሰማይ የዋርሳ

ኩሉ ሓላፋይ
መንከ ተራፋይ
እንታይ ድአስ
ኣይጸገብናያን ንገነት ተስፋይ

133

Kabila

Kabila, Kabila, Kabila.

Who can deny
Kabila, leader of the people,
Got his fill?
His belly testifies.

But I want to know
If his country can grow
On the leftovers.

Kabila, Kabila, Kabila

ካቢላ

ካቢላየ! ካቢላ! ካቢላ! ካቢላ!

አይክተብለካን
እንታይ አልጊልካላ
ከብድኻ ምስክር ባዕላ...

ክብለካ
እንታይ ገዲፍካላ
ክሓልፈላ ዓድኻ ክሓልፈላ...

ካቢላየ! ካቢላ! ካቢላ! ካቢላ!

Tell It Like It Is

Tell it like it is
And the world tells you –
Go to hell.

Cold water
Should be holy
If you throw it
On the *status quo*.

If you make
The world eat dirt,
Call it blessed.
Otherwise,

Tell it like it is
And the world tells you –
Go to hell.

ኣይትፈቱንያ

ኣዱንያ ኣይትፈቱንያ
ዝድርጉሓላ

ማይ ዝሑል ዝነጽገላ
ማይ ጨሎት ዘይብላ

ሓመድ ዘቑኑሕማ
ጸበል እዩ ዘይደግማ

ኣዱንያ ኣይትፈቱንያ
ዝድርጉሓላ

Everybody Hopes

Everybody hopes.
Hopes this, hopes that.
Hopes for, hopes not.

But who helps
Hope?
Is she by herself?
Nope.

"Hey, Fate.
Come here."
Just as we feared.

If hope
Amounts to dust
Nobody trusts
Fate.

ኩልና ብተስፋ

ኩልና ብተስፋ
ኩልና ካብ ተስፋ

ተስፋና በይና ኩይና
ዘብርያ ስኢና
ምስ ዕድል ተላፊና

ተስፋ ጌርና እንተዘይኮይኑልና
ዕድልና እዮ ንብል ዕድልና!

ተስፋ እያ እታ እትውከስ
ዕድል እያ እታ እትውቀስ...በስ!

Life

I define life
As my country:
Birth, spirit,
Struggle, and death.

I define the afterlife
As everybody's country:
Undiscovered,
And nobody's come back yet.

ህይወት

ህይወት አብ ዓድና
ልደት
ኒሕ
ፍኒሕኒሕ
ሞት

ህይወት አብ ዓዲ ኹልና
ሓቢርና ንሕተተላ ሓቢርና

God Gives Us

God gives us
What we have:
Eyes to see,
Ears to hear,
Hearts and minds.

Cruel or kind,
We add, subtract,
Divide and multiply
To tell the truth
From the lie.

God gives us
What we have
And wants us
To return and not to save
What we don't use.

But what are we,
Animals
Created on day five?

ተዋሂቡና እዚ ኹሉ

ዓይኒ ክንርእየሉ
እዝኒ ክንሰምዓሉ
ልቢ ምስ ሓንጎሉ
ክንጭክነሉ/ክንርሕርሓሉ
ክንድምረሉ/ከነጉድለሉ
ክንመቓቐለሉ/ከነርብሓሉ
አስተውዒልና/ክንመምየሉ
አየናይ ሓቂ? አየናይ አሉ?

ተዋሂቡና እዚ ኹሉ
ወይ ንግበረሉ ግብሪ
ወይ ንምለሰሉ ንፈጣሪ

ከይንመልሰሉስ
አንታ ሰብ እንዲና
ምኣስ ፍጥረተ ሓሙስ!

143

No Regrets

Forget Eden.
We're not going back.
Adam and Eve
Had no regrets.

"Good riddance,"
She said.
"So we were fed.
He treated us like animals.
Adam, I love you."

"I love you, too"
He said.
"Nothing beats bread
Baked with your sweat."

Forget Eden.
We're not going back.
Adam and Eve
Had no regrets.

አይተጣዕሱን

አዳምን ሄዋንን
ገነት አይተመልሱን
አይተጣዕሱን

አዳም ሓወይ
እንቂዕ ተረፈና
ዝሃበና ን'ቅበል
እንስሳ ዲና?

ሄዋን ሓብተይ
ዝውሽኽሉ እንተሎ
ዝርሃጽክሉ እንጌራ
ዘመሰሉዋ ዶ'ሎ?

አዳምን ሄዋንን
ገነት አይተመልሱን
አይተጣዕሱን

145

To a Pen

Hey pen,
Please give me a light
For this candle.
Look at that haystack.
Where's the needle?
Look at this other heap
Where Africa is lost
Like a tiny bead of truth
In the sweepings
Of too many limbs and bodies
Hacked by machetes,
Mowed by hunger and disease,
Rotted in jails
And fenced off by oblivion,
When she could be
Happily raising her children.

Please pen,
Give me a light.

አቲ ብርዒ

አቲ ብርዒ እስከ ስምዒ
መወልዒዶ አለኪ መወልዒ?

መውልዕ ሸምዓ
መድለይ ሓቂ
ክንዲ መርፍእ
ክንዲ ዕንቀ
ጠፌኣትኒ አብቲ ሓሰር
ሓሰር አፍሪቃ
ገለን ብጥምየት
ገለን ብሕማም ብማሾስታር
ገለን ብምሳር ብምምታር
ገለን ብምእሳር ገለን ብምሕሳር
ክንዲ ደቃ ምስርሳር

አቲ ብርዒ እስከ ስምዒ
መወልዒዶ አለኪ መወልዒ?

147

The Wheel

White people claim they invented the wheel –
God damned imbeciles!

Have they seen our kitchens?
Look at the oven: a circle,
Whether we cook on metal or clay.
Look at the breads: circles,
Crispy and thin or thick and hard.

Sit down to eat –
Of course, in a circle.
Get up to dance –
In a circle, what else?
Drink too much? Yes, we spin.

Between war and peace, drought and rain,
We've always lived in a vicious circle,
So we invented the wheel

And it's no big deal.
Our ancestors should have invented the car.
We had wheels of barley bread
And local brew like fuel without lead.
Then we would have gone far.

ዕንክሊል

እዚ ፈረንጂ ቀሊልዩ ቀሊል
ምሂዘዮ! ይብል ነቲ ዕንክሊል

አይርአዮን ውሻጠና
ዕንክሊል/መጎጎና
ዕንክሊል/ሞቆሎና
ዕንክሊል/ጣይታና/ሃንዛና
ዕንክሊል/ቅጫና/ጎጎና
ዕንክሊል/ምእድና
ዕንክሊል/ጓይላና
ዕንክሊል/ናብራና
ዕንክሊል/እቲ ሱዋ/ምስ አብዛሕና
ግደፍ በሉዎ ዕንክሊልስ ናህና!

እንተዘስተውዑሉ አቦታትና
ምእተዊ ውሻጠና
ምተማህሩ ካብ አዴታትና
ምስርሑ መኪና
ምተዛወርና! መሽከርከርና!
አርባዕተ ሞጎጎ ሰሪርና
ሱዋ ጸሚቖሩና ንበንዚና!

149

To Our Bread

Taitana, flat face,
Show off your thousand eyes,
Perfect for our sauce
And the curse
Of blindness

ጣይታና

ጣይታና
ክትርኦ ሸሕ ዓይና
ክይትርኢ ተዓዱና
ኣብዚ ሓቶ ዶኾይና?

Eyes in the Front

Eyes in the front of our head,
We never see the future.
Eyes in the front of our head,
We see behind us best.
Eyes in the front of our head
And led by history, forward.

ኣዒንትና ኣብ ቅድሜና

ኣዒንትና ኣብ ቅድሜና
ተፈጢርና
ከይንርኢ መጻኢና
ኣብ ሰማይ ዘሎ ደመና

ኣዒንትና ኣብ ቅድሜና
ተፈጢርና
እቲ እንርእዮ ኣጸቢቕና
ድሕሪና እዩ ታሪኽና

ኣዒንትና ኣብ ቅድሜና
ተፈጢርና
ታሪኽና እዩ ዝመርሓና
ንቕድሜና ንመጻኢና

153

Believe It or Not

Believe it or not,
They want to kill us.

Remember the Italians
Who invaded and said
Eat but don't speak?

Remember the English
Who invaded and said
Speak but don't eat?

Remember the Amharas
Who invaded and said
Don't speak and don't eat?

Still we're shocked
The Weyanes invaded
And said *You should be dead.*

Believe it or not
They want to kill us…

And forced to choose,
We'll always stand
By our martyrs –
No way we'll lose.

እምብዋእ!

ይዝከረኩምዶ ጥልያን መጺኡ
ብልዑ አይትዛረቡ ክብለና?

ይዝከረኩምዶ እንግሊዝ መጺኡ
ተዛረቡ አይትብልዑ ክብለና?

ይዝከረኩምዶ አምሓራ መጺኡ
አይትዛረቡ አይትብልዑ ክብለና?

በሉ ሎምስ ጉድ ሰሚዕና
ጭፍራ ወያነ ጭራሽ አይትንበሩ ክብለና
እምብዋእ! ሎምስ ክኣ ብህይወትና?

በሉ ንትዓወት
ስጋ ስዉኣትና ንማወት
ወይ ናትና ህይወት
ወይ ናቶም ህይወት
ካብ ኮነ ምርጫና
እንመርጾ ንፈልጦ ባዕልና

155

Young and old
Defenders of our land,
I stand with you,
You stand with me,
And God makes three.
Believe it!

ይክአሉ! ዋርሳይ!
አሊኹ ምሳኻ! አሊኻ ምሳይ!
እግዚኣብሔር ሳልሳይ!

157

esh!

The dergue
Behaved better
Than the latest
Swarm of invaders,

Haile Selassie
Better than the dergue,
And Menelik
Better than Selassie.

The progress of Ethiopia
Flows like camel piss:
Backwards.

But my country says
Forward,
And *esh* the Turkish,
esh Egyptians,
esh Italians,
esh the English,

esh Amharas,
esh Tigreans,
esh the locusts.

esh!
Like a flywhisk.

እሺ

ካብ እዚኦምሲ
ደርጊ ይሓይሽ!

ካብ ደርጊ
ሃይለስላሰ ይሓይሽ!

ካብ ሃይለስላሰ
መለሊኻ ይሓይሽ!

ኢትዮጵያ ክትምዕብል
ከም ሽንቲ ገመል ንድሕሪአ ትገይሽ!

ዓደይ ትሓይሽ
ዝዓሰሉዋ እናበለት እሺ!
ንቕድሚአ ትገይሽ

ቱርካዊ   እሺ!
ግብጻዊ   እሺ!
ጥልያን   እሺ!
እንግሊዛዊ   እሺ!
ኣምሓራይ   እሺ!
ትግራዋይ   እሺ!

እሺ! ኣንበጣ ኾማን እሺ!

159

They Don't Eat People?

They don't eat people?
What do you call
Dressing them in rags,
Denying them food and drink,
Seasoning them with hate
And roasting them in the fire?

They don't eat people?
Why all these bones
Where there used to be grain?
Why all that crying out in pain
And so much laughing all night
With the hyenas?

በላዕቲ ሰብ

ለካስ በላዕቲ ሰብ እዮም
አዕሪኾም
አጥሚዮም
አጽሚአም
አብ ሓዊ ጠቢሶም
ክንዲ ጨው በርበረ
ጽልኢ ነስኒሶም

መሬት ደሪኹ / እኽለ ማይ ርሒቑ
ሰብ ኡይ / ዝብኢ እንጉይ / ወያነ ስሓቑ

Vermin

We have all been told
Feed the hungry
Heal the sick.

Blessing the poor,
The leaders
Of too many countries

Also say more:
"Send them to war.
It's efficient.

Death is certain.
Everyone goes,
Fast or slow.

Make it humane.
Sign up and fight.
Understood?"

"No," I say.
What's the logic?
Is death so good?

Life is hard enough.
Does dying make it
Better? *Cui bono?*

ሓሶኻ

ጠምየ ዝበለ
ትምግቦ ኢና ንፈልጥ
ሓሚመ ዝበለ
ትሕክሞ ኢና ንፈልጥ
ህዝቢ ኢትዮጵያ
ኢሉሙ፝ኻዶ ባዕልኻ ትፈልጥ?
ሙማትካ ዘይተርፈካስ
ኣብ ኩናት ይሰልጥ!

ካብ ሞት ድኣ መን ከየምልጥ
ኩሉ ክመውት እዩ ክብል ጭልጥ
እንተ ብትዕግስቲ እንተ ብጽ፝ቅጥቅጥ
ሞይትካስ እንታይ ኢኻሞ ክትባ፝ቝ፝ጥ?

Who benefits
From the remains
But vermin who live off the dead?

ብህይወትካ ዘይከአልካያ ህይወት
ምስ ሞትካስ ነይርሃወት
ምስ ሞትካስ ሓሸኻ እዩ ዝዐወት

I'm Cold

I'm cold
In the hot sun.
I see him,
Deaf and blind.
I see him,
All broken bones,
I see him,
Burned alive.

I'm cold
In the hot sun.
I see him
Dead and not buried.
I see him.
I've cried and cried.
See my berbere eyes.
I see him.

I'm cold
In the hot sun.
I'm sorry,
But what can I say?
Invaders of my country
Always end this way.
I see him
In the hot sun.

እሐው!

እሐው! ፌሪረ
ጽሓይ ከሎ ፌሪረ
ሰብ ርእየ ሰብ ዝነበረ
ሰብ ርእየ ዝጸመመ
ሰብ ርእየ ዝዓወረ
ሰብ ርእየ ምሕሥኹልቱ ዝተሰብረ
ሰብ ርእየ ብህይወቱ ዝሓረረ
ሰብ ርእየ ሞይቱ ዘይተቐብረ

ንብዓተይ ወዲኣ
ኣዒንተይ መሲለን በርበረ
እንታይ እሞ ይገበረ
ንሱ እዩ ትርፉ ዓደይ ዝደፈረ
ንሱ እዩ ትርፉ ዓደይ ዝወረረ

Unless We Know More

We know exactly
Where our enemy is from,

But unless we know more
Hate will make us bitter
And waste our hearts.

Who desecrated
The house of God?
Who ravaged the mosque?
Who plundered the church?
Who gutted our homes
And wanted our families dead?

Will we know the answer?
Can we blame human beings?
Evil spirits not people
Act this way.

But what if the evil spirits say,
"No, we would never do this?"

ጽልኢ ከይነሕድር

ጸላኢ,ና
ዓዱን ዓውዱን
እንዳፈለጥና

ጽልኢ ከይነሕድር
ከይነቓድር ልብና
ቤተ ክርስትያንና
ቤተ እስላምና
ቤተ ሰብና
ቤትና
መን አርከሶ?
መን አፍረሶ?
መን አብረሶ?
ክንሓትት ኢና
መልሱዶ ጢፈኡና
ግዳስ ሰብ አይውዕሉን ኢልና
ገለዶ ደቂ ሕድርትና?

ወሪዱና ደቂ ሕድርትና!
ተውሳኽና! ክሳብ ዝብላና...ኢለናና ኸአ!

Calling the Devil

Our people testify
The enemy gnaws
On our martyrs' bones.

"Peace," you say.
We pray the prayers.
We fast the fasts.

We drink our cup
To the last drop
And keep the faith.

"Deliver us from evil,"
We say, and you promise.

It's time to show up,
Before we're calling the devil.

ሰይጣን ከይጸዋዕና

ጸላእትና ኔው ገጸም
ግሂጸም ሰሚዕና
ኣዕጽም-ቲ ስዉኣትና

ሉቝ ክይንብል
ሰቲናያ ኢና ጽዋእና
ሰቲናያ ጸንቂቝና

ጸዊምና ጸምና
ጸሊና ጸሎትና
ተጸዊትና ኢና ተራና

ኣንታ ፈጣሪ
ተራኻ ግበር
ክፉእ ከይትርኢ

ተራኻ ግበር
ሰይጣን ከይጸዋዕና

Father Noah's Pigeon

Father Noah's pigeon –
Though some call it a dove –
Flew out to see
If the land was safe.

With an olive stalk
Like a toothbrush
In her mouth,
She came back.

Peace and love,
She said, brushing her teeth.
Forget these mountains.
Let's go home, Dad.

If my pet pigeon
Flew to Tigray.
And Showa to ask
"Is there peace?"

Could she escape
All the people
Whose stomach
Is their God?

አቦይ ኖህ ኔራቶ

አቦይ ኖህ ኔራቶ
ርግቢት ድያ ባሬቶ
ዝተላእከቶ

መሬት ዳህሲሳ
መወጽ ንኣፉ
አውሊዕ ቀንጢሳ
ዝተመልሰቶ

አቦይ ኖህ! ዝበለቶ
ጤረር ሜረር አይትፍቶ
ሰላም እያ መሬት ገዛኻ እቶ

እዛ ርግቢተይ ምሰደድኩዋ
ኪዲ ንትግራይ ኪዲ ንሽዋ
እዛ ሰላም ሰላም
ይፈትዉዋ ዶኸን ይፈትዉዋ?

አነስ ምሰደድኩዋ
ከብዶም ዝኣምሳኾም ከይበልዑዋ

Peace Will Come

Peace will come.
From the USA?
No way!
But dream on.

Peace will come.
From the UN?
Are you hallucinating?
Dream on.

Peace will come.
From the OAU?
If wishes were horses.
Dream on.

Peace will come.
From Ethiopia?
Go get 'em.
But dream on.

Peace will come.
From Eritrea?
Where else?
God bless.

ሰላም ክትመጽእ እያ

ሰላም ክትመጽእ እያ
እሰከ ሕለም
ብኣመሪካ
ክላ!

ሰላም ክትመጽእ እያ
እሰከ ሕለም
ብሑቡራት መንግስታት
ክላ ዋእ!

ሰላም ክትመጽእ እያ
እሰከ ሕለም
ብኣፍሪቃ ነገስታት
ክላ ለዓለም!

ሰላም ክትመጽእ እያ
እሰከ ሕለም
ብኢትዮጵያ
ምስ ጸበባ!

ሰላም ክትመጽእ እያ
እሰከ ሕለም
ብኤርትራ
ጸባ ስተ ጸባ!
ሕጃ ኣምጻኻ ዘረባ!

Garden Eritrea

When the blood
Of Eritrean men
Floods Eritrea,
Our heroes grow
Again.

When the blood
Of Eritrean women
Floods Eritrea,
Our heroes grow
Again.

When the blood
Of Eritreans
Floods Eritrea,
We grow back
Again and again.

Deny peace
To Eritrea
And you garden
Eritreans.

ይኹስከሰና

አብ ኤርትራ ዓድና
ፈሰሰት ደምና
ርሓሰት መሬትና
ፈረየት ስብኡትና

እንደገና!

አብ ኤርትራ ዓድና
ፈሰሰት ደምና
ርሓሰት መሬትና
ፈረየት አንስትና

እንደገና!

አብ ኤርትራ ዓድና
ፈሰሰት ደምና
ርሓሰት መሬትና
ፈረየት ወረስትና

ተረዲኡና!

አብ ኤርትራ ዓድና
ሰላም ጋኸልአና
ይኹስከሰና ማለት·ዩ

177

Plant Our Feet

We're pushed with
"Your neighbors deny
The truth so easily,
So why can't you?"

True.
They'll say anything –
"Let earth be sky,
Let sky be earth"
And hang upside down.

But we look straight,
Say, "Look. The sky above,
The earth below
And the good and bad
In between"
And plant our feet.

እግርና ተኰልና

አይስአኑን ዝብሉ
ንሓቂ በሉ አሉ
ንጕረቤትኩም ምሰሉ

ሰማይ መሬት መሬት ሰማይ
ምባሉ ቀሊል እዩ
አለዉ ኽኣ ዝብሉ
ቀኑልቀኑል አፍም ክሳብ ዝትከሉ

ከማና ዝአመሰሉ
ንሰማይ ሰማይ ንመሬት መሬት ይብሉ
ጽቡቕ አሉ ክፉእ አብ ማእከሉ
እግርና ተኰልና ቀኔዕና ንዓጥቀሉ

UCPP

The United Children of Pontius Pilate
Wash their hands of truth and ask "What is it?"
Did they save Christ? Wasn't he innocent?
Why should Eritrea's fate be different?
United and condemning everyone,
They throw justice to the dogs like a bone.
God save us, weak or strong, from these cowards
Who lead with eyes and ears under bandages of power.

ነገደ ጲላጦስ

ነገደ ጲላጦስ
እንተተተድሕኑ
መድሓንኩም ክርስቶስ

ማይ ትሕጸቡ ምኣስ ክትበልዑ
ከተብልዑ ወዲ ሰብ ምስ ርትዑ

ኤርትራ
ነፊዓ ሓሚቓ
ብዘይካ ኣምሳኻ የብላን ሓለቓ

ሓቢርኩም ዘይተድሕኑ
ሓቢርኩም ችሹንኑ

ንመንከ ከይተሕብሩ?
ዓይንኹም እዝኚኹም
ብጨርቂ ተኾኒኑ

181

Ruff! Ruff!

Communitas made plain
Is Eritrean:
A hungry brother there
Means I don't eat here.

Communitas made plain
Explains Eritrea:
A thirsty sister there
Means I don't drink here.

Does this basic tie offend
The new American way
Of markets without end
And being what you buy?

Do they call their friends
Because we don't buy enough
And give to each other
To provide?
They threaten us, "Ruff! Ruff!"

But whose bark or bite
Scares Eritreans,
At home and worldwide
Tied together so tight?

ዉሕ! በሉዋ ንኤርትራ

ማሕበራዊ ናብራ
ናይ ኤርትራ
ሓወይ ጠምዩ
እንታይ ኢለዮ እንጌራ

ማሕበራዊ ናብራ
ናይ ኤርትራ
ሓብተይ ጸሚኣ
ኣነ እውን ከምኣ

ነዚኣ ርእያ
ኣመሪካ ኮርያ
ማሕበራዊ ናብራ
ንዕዳጋይ ሸኾራ

ኢላቶም ንኮራኹራ
ዉሕ! በሉዋ ንኤርትራ
ማሕበራዊ ናብራ ከይነብራ

ኣሸንኳይ ዉሕ ኢሎማ ናሺሶማ
ኤርትራ ኣይትገድፍን ማሕበራዊ ማእለማ
ንሓንቲ ባንዴራ ንሓንቲ ሰንደቕ ዕላማ

The Visit

Mrs. Albright?
The Mrs. Albright
With all the power and right?
Why can't you
Shine in Africa?

Mrs. Albright?
Please, I'll make you coffee
And burn incense –
Kofi Annan can have some, too –
For the devil in you:
Letting you only see white
When you want to save a life.

Mrs. Albright?
It is Mrs. Albright,
Not all dark,
Right?

ወይዘሮ ኩሉ-ብርሃን

ወይዘሮ ኩሉ-ብርሃን
ምስዚ ኹሉ ስልጣን
ኃኻልእ ድኣ እምበር
ንኣፍሪቃስ መኻን

ወይዘሮ ኩሉ-ብርሃን
ክጨልወልክን ቡን
ክትጸበልክን ዕጣን
ክደግመልክን ድጋም
ዘህድም ሰይጣን
ዘብለክን እወ
ይጥፋእ ዝይጸዕደወ
ከም ኮፈ ኣናን

ወይዘሮ ኩሉ-ብርሃን
ጸልሚቲክንዶ
ጸልሚቲክንዶ
ንዓኽን ከማን

On Her Watch

Eagle-eyed Albright
Watches day and night,
Ready to call security.
She sees famine and war
Faraway in Africa – a pity,
But what is Africa for?

At ease.

ሽላ እያ ሽላ!

ወይዘሮ ኩሉብርሃን
ዓለም ትሕሉ ኣላ
ሽላ እያ ሽላ!
ይብሃል

ኣፍሪቃ ጸሚኣ
ኣፍሪቃ ጠምያ
ኣፍሪቃ ሓሚማ
ኣፍሪቃ ትዋጋእ ኣላ
ኣፍሪቃ! ኣፍሪቃ! ንዝብላ...

ክላ በጃኻ ክላ!
ኣፍሪቃስ ኣመላ እዩ ኣመላ!

187

Bush Afrique

Hyenas like
Bush.
More social animals,
We read the Bible,
Play "Hail to the Chief"
And pray
Bush
Stays away
From hyenas.

ገረብ ስሙ።

ሰብ ናብ ሰቡ
ከም ቀደሙ።

ዝብኢ ናብ ገረቡ
ከም ቀደሙ።

አቦይ ቀሺ
ዳዊትኩም ድገሙ።

ገረብ ከይበሃል
ናብ ዝብኢ ሰጕሙ።

ንጉስ አመሪካ
ገረብ ስሙ።

189

Exposure

Away from Asmara in Brussels
In the cold of early winter
I saw her standing outside
With her clothes piled at her feet:

Naked as the day she was born,
A descendent of African trees,
No longer able to bear fruit,
Stripped of her leaves and exposed.

I worried but was reassured.
In this culture she was supposed
To shed her dress in the cold
And put it back on in spring.

Trees change their ways or die
Under foreign skies.

ጥራሕ ካን ጥራሕ

ብራስልስዩ ከይመስለኩም አስመራ
ክረምቲ እዩ መሬት ጨሪራ
ዝርኣኹዋ ግዳም ተገቲራ
ክዳውንታ አብ እግራ ኮሚራ

ጥራሕ ካን ጥራሕ
ከምዛ አዲአ ዝወለደታ
ዳዕሮ ትመስል ንሳግላ ሓውታ
ጨጽሊ እኳ የብላን ንሕፍረታ
አይብላዕን ኢሎሞ ፍርያታ

አነ ተሻቒላ ብናታ
ከምኡ እዩ ኢሎመኒ ባህርያታ
ሓጋይ ሓጋይ ትወድየን ክዳውንታ
ክረምቲ መጸ ትድርብየን ከምዛይናታ

አግራብ ኩለን ጠባየን አይሓደን
ገሊኤንስ ገደደን አብ ዘይዓደን

191

Hey, Constitution

Hey, Constitution,
Blood of my blood,
What's happening?

You're on the road too long.
You've almost made it home.
Why have you stopped
At a man's house?
Do you want to be there
Or does he make you stay?
Send word.

Hey, Constitution,
My reason for living,
What's happening?

Come live with me,
Home for good,
Show me the way.
Name the time: winter or spring,
Eritrean style or European,
It'll be like New Year's day.

Hey, Constitution,
Blood of my blood,
What's happening?

ቅዋመይ

ቅዋመይ
መንቀጽ ደመይ
ከመይ ከመይ?

ቀሪብኪ ኔርኪ ክትኣትዊ ዓዲ
ትኽ ኢልኪ ከይቶኸሲ
ተኣሊኺ እንዳ እቲ ወዲ
ፈቲኽዮ ዲኺ ብግዲ?

ደንጉኺ ኣብ መገዲ
እስከ ድሃይ ስደዲ

ቅዋመይ
ፈውሲ ሕማመይ
ከመይ ከመይ?

ኣይቆቡዕ ኣይሮቡዕ
ንዒ እባ ሓዳር ግበሪ
ንዒ እባ ኣመሓድሪ
ንዒ መስከረም ንዒ ጥሪ
ብፈረንጇ ዲኺ ብሓበሻ ትቖጽሪ?

ቅዋመይ
መንቀጽ ደመይ
ከመይ ከመይ?

Freedom of Speech

Like animals
People can agree.
But to argue
Seriously or for fun
We have speech.

If we fail
To keep it free,
Not giving everyone,
A say, remember
Babel – it fell.

ናይ ሰብ ነገር

ናይ ሰብ ነገር
ከም እንስሳ ይትሓባበር
እንስሳ እዩ ይዛረብ ኩይኑ እምበር

ይዛረብ ይናገር
ገለ ዋዛ ገለ ቄምነገር
ይሰርሕ ገዛ ይምስርት ሃገር

ሰሚዕኩምዶ ባቤል ክዓኑ
ንዘረባ መዛረቢ ምስ ስእኑ

High and Low

The word from on high
Descends, but from whom?

The people tower above,
The government dwells below.

The government towers, too,
But not as high as the people.

God dwells where he wills.

The word from on high,
Descends, but from whom?

ላዕልን ታሕትን

ካብ ላዕሊ እዮ መጺኡ
ካብ መን ድኣ እዮ?

ህዝቢ እዮ ላዕሊ
መንግስቲ ትሕቲኡ

መንግስቲ እዮ ላዕሊ
ህዝቢ ልዕሊኡ

እግዚኄር ጥራይ እዮ
ከም ድላዩ

ካብ ላዕሊ እዮ መጺኡ
ካብ መን ድኣ እዮ?

197

A One Man Show

With so much to do
God had to divide
Himself into three:
Father, Son, and Holy Ghost.

On the sixth day
God created Adam.
Working all alone
Bent the man too low.

He was lost until
God took Adam's bone,
Made Eve,
And put both in the saddle.

Our ancestors say
If you have one eye,
Be careful out there,
And if you have one ox,
You have none to spare.

ሐደ ንበይኑ

አምላኽ ባዕሉ
ከርክበሉ ኝኹሉ
ሐደ ኣካሉ
ኣብ ሰለስተ ከፊሉ
ኣብ
ወልድ
መንፈስ ቅዱስ ተባሂሉ

ከምኡ ውን ንኣዳም
ምስ ፈጠሮ ቀዳም
ሐደ ንበይኑ
ኣርዑት ከቢዱዋ
ምስ ረአዮ ደኒኑ
ምስ ሄዋን ጸመዶ ብእዋኑ

ናይ ኣቦታት ክጠቅስ
ብዓል ሐደ ብዕራይ ኣይለግስ
ብዓል ሐደ ዓይኒ ኣይገስግስ

Dear Hand

Dear Hand,
Before you act
Ask
Eye,
Ear,
Brain
And heart
What they would make
And join it
To your plan.
They'll say
"We have a hand"
In what you create
And "Give it a hand"
To praise your art.

ኢድ

ኢድ ተጣበቢ
ቅድም ተላዘቢ
ምስ ዓይኒ
ምስ እዝኒ
ምስ ቀልቢ
ምስ ልቢ

አየ ኢድ! እንተበለኺ
ምአስ ንበይንኺ!

Eyes

People have two eyes.
Light lets me see
The world, but nature
Won't let my eyes
See themselves
Except with a mirror.
But what do I see?
It can't compare
With being told
You are my eyes.
People need each other –
When I see my eyes and me
In the eyes of another
And when they want to see
The way I see, too,
We can lead each other home
To our one humanity.

ዓይኒ

ከም ሰበይ
በዓል ክልተ ዓይኒ
ዓለም በሪሁስ ይርኣየኒ
በዒንተይ ብናተይ
ከይርኢ ኣዒንተይ
ኣይፈቅድን ፍጥረተይ

መስትያት ውን ኣለኒ
ክንዲ ሰብ ነይኮኑኒ
ኣታ ዓይነይ! ዝብለኒ

ሰብ ንሰብ ይደሊ ብፍጥረቱ
ኣዒንቱ ክርኢ በዒንቲ ኣሕዋቱ
ኣሕዋቱ ክርእዩ በዒንቱ
ተመራሪሑ ዓዲ ክኣቱ
ናይ ሰብ ሓድነት እንሆ ብልሃቱ

Hearts

Our citizen hearts cover the range.
Relaxed, they settle down.
Sick, they spout fire.
Fading and almost gone,
They pump back up like balloons.

Bizarre and full of change,
Our citizen hearts require
That we act on our wisest desire:
Two hearts together
Beat better than one.

ልቢ

ልቢ ደቂ ዓደይ ጉዳመኛ
ትሃድእ/ትረግእ
ትሓምም/ትሓርር
ትመሎኽ/ትጠፍእ
ትንፋሕ/ከም ፍሒኛ

በዓል ሓደ ልቡ
ክንብለካ ብልብና
ልቢ ግበር ልቦና
ልብኻ ሃብና ክንህበካ ልብና
ለበዋ ለባማትና

Y2K

Who knows how
Old or young
The world really is?

But asking her age
Means more
Than checking her teeth
Like a donkey.

I can celebrate
Two millennia
Of being created
To live, raise hell,
Roll in it, cry
Enough and die
So the love of Jesus
Can forgive me.
But what about before?

I better count again
And this time be less vain.

ክልተ ሽሕ

ዓለም ካብ ትፍጠር
ይንዋሕ ይሕጸር
ኣይፍለጥን ይጥርጠር

ሰብ እዩ ጠርጣሪ
ኣስናና ቄጻሪ
ሸረፍ ጕረፍ
ገልገለ ሂለለ
ምስ ኣድጊ ኣነጻጻሪ

ክልተ ሽሕ ዘኽብሩ
እንታይ ምስ ቄጸሩ?

ሰብ ተፈጢሩ
ኣብ ዓለም ሰፊሩ
ኣዕገርጊሩ ኣንገርጊሩ
ምስ ጸገበስ
ክንዲ ዝቐጸዐ ተማሒሩ
ብእየሱስ ክርስቶስ መምህሩ

ሰብ ሰብ ኩይኑ
ንዓይ ጥራይ ተኸናኸኑ!

To the Real, New Millennium

To God we say
"Thy will be done"
And to the president
"Our will be done"

In the hope that one
Will bow our way,
And even then,
Africa's children,

We know
We'll sweat our brow
For whatever we get.

Should we bet
You'll deliver, 2001?

ክልተ ሽሕናን እንኮናን

ፍቓድካ ይኹን!
ንግዚሄርና
ፍቕድና ይኹን!
ንርእሰ ብሄርና

ካብ ክልቲአም ሓዲአም
ወስ ክብሉ ግደአም
ትጽቢትና

አፍሪቃውያን ኢና
ዝጉዶለ እንተሎ
ንምልአ ርኒጽና

ክልተ ሽሕን እንኮን
ችኹኒ ዶኾን
ክልተ ሽሕናን እንኮናን?

Snails, Men

Snails, that is, men
Poking along not knowing
Thieves took their cattle
And only a sword
Can bring them back again
From America, Europe, Asia and Australia:
Our brightest children taken,
Their faces flush with dollars.
And the thieves return.
Pretending to be poor
They empty our shelves
And suck the remains
Down to our bones and marrow.
Too slow, we are forsaken
If we don't move fast,
Feeding the people we still have
Like fire and bringing home
The beautiful future we let go.
Choose your weapon.
If we know what we endure
We know the cure.

እረነ! እረነ!

እረነ! እረነ!
አሓ እንዳቦኻ
አሓ እንዳደኻ ተዘሚተንየ
ንዓባ ጕራደ ጌራካ አምጽአየን አምልሰንየ

በዓል አመሪካ እንታይ ገደሰን
ብዓል እስያ እንታይ ገደሰን
ብዓል ኤውሮጳ እንታይ ገደሰን
ደላር አብ ቅድሚአም ከስኪሰን
ምሁራት አሓዋትካ
ወሲደን ሓፊሰን
ዘይዑናኻ ዑና መን አብሪሰን?

ክወርዳ እየን ዕዳጋ ተመሊሰን
ጥሙያት ስሱዓት ንሰን
ናተን ሓቢአን ብናትካ ከሪሰን
ሓዊ እምበር ሓውኺ አይተኾሉልሰን

ምስ አሕዋትካ ምኽረሉ
አምልሰም አምልሰን ተጣበበሉ
ንዘመናዊ ውግእ ዘመናዊ ጕራደ ፍጠረሉ
ሕማሙ ዝፈለጠ አይስእንን ጸበሉ

211

The Graceful

Graceful
Gatherers and hunters
Wearing bandoleers,
White netselas* or suits,
Should we build a nation
Or forget about it?

Whom should we satisfy?
Whom should we deny?
Who deserves our praise?
Whom should we condemn
For our heap of problems?
We either decide

Our future together
Or hate and bore each other.
No more limits
To what we think
In love or fear.
We should not forget about

Our nation but build it,
As each of us knows how,
Assuring in the end
That everyone has a share
And adds a prayer
For peace in our land.

*traditional cloak

ተሸዋኖ

አቲም ደቂ ዓደይ ተሸዋኖ
አቲም ሰብ ዝናር አቲም ሃዳኖ
አቲም ሰብ ሽርጥ ሰብ ነጸላ ሰብ ባኖ
እዛ ዓድና ትልማዕዶ ትዕኖ

ንመንኩም ከሐጉስ
ንመንኩም ከሕዝኖ
ንመንኩም ክውድስ
ንመንኩም ክኮንኖ
ቶኾሚሩሎ ናይ ዓድና ተጽዕኖ

አይንጻላእ አይንማኖ
ናይ ዓድና መጻኢ
ብሓንሳእ ንወስኖ

ይደርንሕ ይፈኖ
ናይ ሓሳባት መስኖ
ንመን አብዩ ንመን ከይኮኖ

ትልማዕ አይትዕኖ
ንከፋፈል እጃምና ባዕልና ንውንኖ
ብዘተርፈ ንዝጊ ንለምንኖ
አብቲ ዓድና ሰላም ከስፍኖ

213

We're Talking Back

One of us
Equals more than some?
Some of us
Equal more than everyone?

Do you multiply
And plus
Or divide
And take away
From us?

Can this be the right amount?

We're talking back,
But still you continue to count.
(We're also keeping track,
But in our hearts.)

ድአ በልና

ሓዴና'ዶ ይበዝሕ ገሌና?
ገሌና'ዶ ይበዝሕ ኩልና?
ኩልና'ዶ ይበዝሕ ሓዴና?
ሓቲትና

ክንድምርዶ ከነጉድል ከለና?
ከነርብሕዶ ክንመቅል ከለና?
ተሓቲትና

ስጋኹም ስጋ ሓድነትና!
ደምሩና አይተጉድሉና!
አርብሑና አይትምቀሉና!
ድአ በልና

ቁጽሪ ዝይፈልጡ ቁጽርና
ኮይኖም ተቜጻጺርትና
(አስዒብና ብልብና)

The Transit of Tigrinya

For her the seas connect.
The mountains increase her reach.
She moves fast.
But what did you assume
About Tigrinya?

Eritrea's daughter,
She wants respect,
The same as you.
Dare her,
She'll dare you, too.

She knows the way
To overcome
The invading tongues:
Her words, her names
Cut them off.

The world may ask why,
But now it hears her glory.
Rome invited her first
To sing, and New York,
Rome's Rome, will bring

Her with Reesom
And the Virgin Mary
To join, *gTmi* – make Tigrinya
Poetry the joy
Of all the city's girls and boys.

እንታይ እዋና?

እንታይ እዋና ባሕሪ ሰጊራ
እንታይ እዋና ነቦ ተጊራ
ይብሃል ድዩ ንንጏል ኤርትራ

ትግርኛ ንጏል ሃገራ
ሓፋር ንዝሓፍራ
ደፋር ንዝደፍራ
ብኽንደይ ኛታት ተወሪራ
ልሳና ብልሳና አውጺአ ሓራ
ዓለም ገራሙዋ ምስጢራ
ጀሚራ አላ ጀሚራ ከተኽብራ

ሰሚዕኩምዶ
ሮማ ክትዕድማ?
ተዓዲማ ሎሚ ድማ
ብናይ ሮማ ሮማ...ኒው ዮርክ
ክትደግም ድጋማ
ክትገጥም ግጥማ
ተሰንያ ብማርያማ
ተዓጂባ ብርእሰማ
ሃነን ከተብሎም ንደቂ ኸተማ...ኒው ዮርክ

217

New York be the judge.
Tigrinya has no fear.
A shout out to English.
Join Tigrinya's z-ezm,
Z-ezm or disappear.

ሰሚዕኪዶ እንግሊዝኛ?
ንዕናይ ነው ዮርክ አብ ዳኛ
ወይ ዝ-እዝም በሊ ከም ትግርኛ
ወይ ህልም በሊ ከም ቀኈንቀኈኛ

Family Name?

She asks my name,
And I tell her.
"No," she says,
"Your family name.
Do you have one?"

One what?
One name? One family?
I told her my name.
I know my father's name,
My grandfather's
And all the names
Back seven generations.

What does she want?
One name for all my family?
That makes no sense,
But maybe I should claim

"Eritrea."
I'm her son, and my parents
Are Eritrea's children, too.
"Family name?" she says again.
"Eritrea," I respond.
"Hello, Mr. Eritrea. How are you?"

ሽም ስድራይዶ?

መን ሽምካ ኢላትኒ
ሽመይ ሒበያ
ሽም ስድራኻ ኢላትኒ
ሽም ስድራይዶ?

ሽም ስድራዶ የብልካን ኢኻ?

ኣነ እምብኣር ዝፈልጦ
ሽምካ/ሽም ኣቦኻ/ሽም ኣቦሓጎኻ
ክሳብ ሾውዓተ ወለዶኻ
እንታይ እያ እዛ ሽም ስድራኻ?

ኣሃ...ሕጂ ፈሊጠያ
ኣነ ወዲ ኤርትራ
ስድራይ ደቂ ኤርትራ
ኤርትራ እንድያ ሽም ስድራይ...
ሽም ስድራይስ ኤርትራ በልያ ኢለያ

ዘይመስላ ብዘይካ ከም ሃገራ
ክትብለኒ እንድያ ሃሎዉ! ሚስተር ኤርትራ!
ዋዛዶ ሎኒ እዮ ወዲ ኤርትራ
ይርኣየኒሎ ኣቤት ክብላ ብስም ስድራ

221

Four Dots ::

Four dots
Demarcate
Tigrinya sentences
Like the lock
On a border gate.

Four dots
::
Pin east, west, north and south
To one spot.
Writing and mouth
Stop.

ኦርባዕተ ኖቑጣ

ጽሑፍና
ደረቱ ከይሓልፍ
ንምብራኽ
ንምዕራብ
ንሰሜን
ንደቡብ
ከይብለና ህትፍ
ብኦርባዕተ ኖቑጣ ንቑልፍ
፣፣

ኣጽቅጥ ንዝልፍልፍ
ኦርባዕተ ኖቑጣ ንዝጽሕፍ

Afterword

The Poetry of Reesom Haile

Charles Cantalupo

I

Reesom Haile considers his writing in Tigrinya

A going back to what God has given you and saying "I'm not going to give it up." It's your freedom, your speech, your self-definition, and your self-expression. You cannot give it up. If you lose your language, it isn't just the language you lose. It's the cultural codes imbedded in that language. It's the values, the sense of community, and the sense that I am responsible for my brother, my sister, my mother, and they are equally responsible to me. This is what I do not want my people to lose.

Reesom Haile also writes in a spirit that is inseparable from Eritrea's century-long struggle for independence. In his own words,

> The Eritrean struggle for independence is the primary motive force for my art....We Eritreans have taken on all comers for our right to self-determination, and my art is but a continuation and an expansion of that struggle aimed at self-definition.

Eritrea's war for independence was simultaneously a war for its culture: its ancient traditions as well as its modern manifestations and transformations. Again in Reesom Haile's words,

> Successive enemies of Eritrean independence over the years have tried defining Eritrea in ways that would justify the outrageous measures they would take to deny Eritrea its place in the sun. They have tried to diminish Eritrea politically, economically, militarily, and culturally into non-existence except as an appendage of the builders of colonial and neo-colonial empires. But Eritrea has proved a survivor....

War as a cultural education towards making peace requires not only the barrel of a gun but also the barrel of a pen, as Ngugi wa Thiong'o observes. The cultural bomb can be as deadly as bombs falling from the sky. What is in the mind of the person holding the gun and pulling the trigger? The fighter and the writer not only need each other. They are often the same person – and always the same person in spirit. As Reesom Haile also recalls:

I returned to Eritrea in 1994 after twenty years of life in exile. I came back to find our languages and our poetry a bit battered, but well, considering they too had been targeted for extinction....But we carried our languages and our art in our memories and our voices, and we used them as effectively as we used our weapons to defend ourselves throughout the struggle.

Vitally linked, Reesom Haile's language of self-determination and political self-determination produce a supreme poetry of resistance with the confidence to ask,

> But what did you assume
> About Tigrinya?
>
> Eritrea's daughter,
> She wants respect,
> The same as you.
> Dare her,
> She'll dare you, too.
>
> She knows the way
> To overcome
> The invading tongues:
> Her words, her names
> Cut them off.
>
> ("The Transit of Tigrinya")

A local language and its poetry become the means of survival:

> Remember the Italians
> Who invaded and said
> *Eat but don't speak?*

Remember the English
Who invaded and said
Speak but don't eat?

Remember the Amharas
Who invaded and said
Don't speak and don't eat?
...
Believe it or not,
They want to kill us...

("Believe It or Not")

Poetry of resistance is inseparable from the life of the poet
and his country:

The dergue
Behaved better
Than the latest
Swarm of invaders,

Haile Selassie
Better than the dergue,
And Menelik
Better than Selassie.
...
But my country says
Forward,
And *esh* the Turkish,
esh Egyptians,
esh Italians,
esh the English,
esh Amharas,
esh Tigreans,
esh the locusts.

esh!

Like a flywhisk.

("esh!")

While focusing on and from Eritrean culture, Reesom Haile's poetry of resistance also has a global dimension as a part of, again in his words, "the indomitable struggle of humanity." He has a self-stated "mission...to create links between my country and the world." Celebrating a "genuine," "Eritrean culture" that expresses "the essence of human struggle," as he sees it, his poetry can simultaneously partake of a literary impulse that is universal, making a literary truism breathe new life. His "imagination" with his "poet's pen," in Shakespeare's words, "bodies forth / The forms of things unknown." He "[t]urns them to shapes, and gives to aery nothing / A local habitation and a name." But if the habitation is African, let the name be African. Let the word itself and the word "language" in African languages ring out all over Africa: *Mutauro, Ulwimi, Edi, Okasa, Asusu, Lolemu, Ulimi, Lakk, Ruthiomi, Lugha, Harsha, Luqha, Qwanqwa.* They are the medium *and* they are the message, adding up to Africa's greatest expression of freedom: *Amandla!* The resounding African word is universally understood – as if the story of Babel and the confusion of tongues were not true – by people of all walks of life, all ages and in many languages, local and international, from under the giant Sycamore trees of arid Eritrea to the elegant arts venues of downtown New York City; from the poor, local communities of Johannesburg, South Africa, or Newark, New Jersey to the halls of the world's most distinguished universities.

No one cultivates freedom in Tigrinya and the "local habitation" in Eritrea better than Reesom Haile does. As in the first bilingual collection of his poems, *We Have Our Voice*, the poetry of *We Invented the Wheel* presents a myriad of subjects, including: bread, marital responsibility, competition, snails, American foreign policy, democracy, women's rights, global politics, casualties of war, love, the young, elders, the nature of advice, spousal abuse, cooking, cannibalism, coffee, self-image, sleeping together, proverbs, ethnic conflict, carousing, biblical stories, tourism, national identity, aging, values, the future, the pen, words, exile, shoes, masculinity, teaching babies to walk, videos of weddings, religious hypocrisy, history, body parts, suicide, funerals, taboos, freedom, independence, infidelity, flywhisks, community, temptation, unspeakable evil, spirits, old and new housing, frankness, circles, sex, labor, ancestors, mothers, prayers, parenting, toys, food, starvation, war, donkeys, the millennium, Jews, Muslims, Christians, punctuation, political evil, weather, onomatopoeia, loss, wisdom, literature, peace, jokes, teachers, culture, hierarchy, individualism, letters, pastry, paper, poverty, hope, surnames, God, George Bush II, sacrifice, survival, African leaders, dictators, devils, language, relationships, regrets, dependable people, dissent, angels, and home. If there has ever been a poetry with something for everyone, this is it: which accounts for the great popularity of Reesom Haile's poetry in Eritrea, yet which is now a major factor in his increasing, international acclaim.

II

Writing in Tigrinya, Reesom Haile joins a growing movement of African authors who are now writing in African languages: their own mother tongues instead of colonial languages like English and French or, in the case of Eritrean writers, Italian and even Amharic, a major language of Ethiopia imposed on Eritrea before it won its war for independence in 1991. This rise of African vernaculars, paralleling the rise of truly independent and democratic African nations, promises a 21st century that will be an African century for literature.

European literature's takeover by vernacular languages took place so long ago that few but medieval and classical students and scholars want to or even can read the thousands of years of writing in Latin and Greek that preceded it. Yet the European Renaissance precisely paralleled the rise of European languages other than Greek and Latin. Furthermore, the European Renaissance was inconceivable without the growth and development of vernacular languages, not only in literature and the arts, but also in science, government, politics, philosophy, religion, education, medicine, economics, social and personal development. Readers who limited themselves to authors writing in Latin, would have missed the likes of Dante, Chaucer, Rabelais, Shakespeare, Cervantes and many others writing in their own vernaculars – and this was only the *literature* that would have been missed. To live during the European Renaissance and to miss these writers and the wealth of other written activity and information in European vernaculars at the time would have been to miss the life of the Renaissance itself. European vernaculars were, of course, always in use in everyday European life by everyone nearly all the time, but to have missed its representation in those same languages would have reflected a debilitating, exclusive aesthetic, language philosophy or policy that did, after all, prove fatal. Again, who of real or lasting intellectual importance was reading and writing only in Latin or Greek by the end of the European Renaissance?

Readers and listeners today who are limited to African writers in English, French or other Europhone languages risk being similarly cut off, even though great African writers continue working in these languages and are second to none in developing them. But African writers have many, many more languages than Europhone languages – African languages. African writers also have many, many more readers in African languages – African readers. African literature cannot and will not exclude but accepts and continues to rejoice in African writers in Europhone languages because the reality of Africa means that they are African, too. Yet great African languages like Yoruba, Zulu, Swahili, Gikuyu, Hausa, Akan, Amharic, Tigrinya, hundreds and thousands more require what Europhone readers have not previously needed to read great contemporary African literature – *translators*. This new and widespread need for translators of contemporary African language writing should not be surprising. It follows a familiar, historical pattern and a natural need. As Ngugi wa Thiong'o observes, African language writers "see their role as that of doing for African languages and cultures what all writers and intellectuals of other cultures and histories have done for theirs."

Thousands of African languages, ancient and modern, are spoken and / or written locally, regionally, nationally and internationally. As Ludwig Wittgenstein famously states, "To imagine a language means to imagine a form of life," and surely no language is an exception. Each is like a human being with his or her own complex biology, even including a kind of verbal genome. Would anyone who contends that some languages are not vitally important because they are spoken by too few people from tiny geographical places say the same about similarly sized and remote cultures that originated the Old and New Testaments of the Bible, or the manuscripts of Homer and Sophocles? Where or what would Europhone languages and cultures be – including their profound extensions in North and South America – without their translations of these texts from locales and populations that are small by contemporary and even ancient standards? The answer is inconceivable. The influence of such texts, however humble their origins, is ubiquitous, practically timeless and inseparable from any sense of self, soul, state or the beyond precisely because these texts have been willingly, eagerly and frequently translated. Reverenced in the original and translated continually, they create a desire for lifelong learning. To turn to African language writings, the rewards of their translation are considerable, and the promise of their originals is greater still.

The simplest, most economic, applicable, neglected, democratic, holistic and achievable way to improve African lives and livelihoods through the application of knowledge, science, technology, research and analysis is the empowerment of African languages. The vitality and equality of African languages should be recognized as the basis for the future empowerment of African people. African languages, including their translation into each other and into other world languages, offer *the* alternative vision of development in Africa, establishing African languages as a primary source for traditional and future social change, economic development and individual self-realization in Africa's 21st century. The incongruity of only colonial-derived languages speaking for the African continent is unacceptable. At the start of a new century and millennium, African-language writers reject this incongruity and affirm a new beginning by returning to their own mother tongues. Furthermore, the question of culture, literatures and languages cannot be separated from the economic problems caused by colonial and neocolonial forces and their local allies. Realism and pragmatism dictate the teaching and use of international languages like French or English and others. But how can they connect and not disconnect – with all of their resources and information – with the vast majority except through their own, mother tongues? As European vernacular languages fed a vast array of creative fires that burning into each other became the European Renaissance, so the African Renaissance simply and directly addresses the most basic demand and reaches out to a natural constituency of writers, teachers, readers and speakers in local languages – the vast majority of Africans – to encourage and enable all kinds of information dissemination in African languages. They are the keys to the development of a culture of peace and prosperity in Africa. Their diversity reflects the rich cultural heritage of Africa itself and is the primary instrument for African unity.

A mirror image of Africa itself, African languages have had to struggle "against all odds" to be heard in education, political and social policy, government and the arts, where non-African languages generally are dominant. For example, other than for Arabic, a language of northern and other parts of Africa, no other African language is spoken in the Security Council of the United Nations. Even the Organization of African Unity (OAU) used no others, though hopefully its replacement, the African Union, will? This silencing of African languages has resulted in the disempowerment of the vast majority of Africans, precisely because they do not speak non-African languages: the same Africans who are always the first and most long-suffering victims of war, poverty, epidemic, famine and other catastrophes. People speaking and hearing for themselves in their own mother tongues are the greatest force for peace and development. The exclusion of African languages from African political, social, economic, educational and personal development is an aggressive act against African people. Language rights are a part of human rights, too. How else are they honestly to be stated, communicated and understood? – especially by the vast majority of people in Africa who simply do not speak French or English. As Ngugi wa Thiong'o asks, "If some of the best and most articulate of the interpreters of African total being insist on interpreting in languages not understood by the subject of their interpretation, where lies the hope of African deliverance?"

234

Tigrinya is a Semitic language and, like the languages of Tigre and Amharic, derives from the ancient language of Ge'ez. It derives, like Hebrew and Arabic, from Aramaic, which is often thought to have been a language – along with Greek and Hebrew – of the original composition of much of the Old and New Testament and of Jesus.

While Tigrinya is a major language of Eritrea, Eritrea has no one official language but officially recognizes nine languages. These nine languages are the basis of a progressive mother-tongue education system in Eritrea, which continues up to the fifth grade. Also, news reports, judicial proceedings and government programs and documents function in all nine languages. Obviously such a policy is not without its political and economic difficulties, but it is based on the simple and imperative realization that if the language of any group of people – however small in population – is not recognized, then the people themselves will not be recognized, leading to injustice and inequality if they are to try to participate and be represented in a democratic society. South Africa has a similarly progressive language policy, having mandated that its new Constitution exists in ten languages.

Contrary to the idea that translation, by growing an audience, hastens the demise of mother tongues, international or global recognition and translation have enhanced and not endangered Reesom Haile's poetry in Tigrinya. Preceding *We Invented the Wheel*, *We Have Our Voice* was the first bilingual book of Tigrinya / English poetry. No Tigrinya poet before Reesom Haile has had such widespread media attention – including *BBC* (UK), *CNN* (USA), *Deutche Welle* (Germany), *RAI* (Italy), *dmtsi Hafash* (Eritrea) *Radio Vatican* (The Vatican), *NPR* (USA),

SABC (South Africa), *SBS* (Australia) and *VOA* (USA) – publications and critical analysis in as many distinguished literary journals. He has been translated into ten languages and has been invited to read throughout Africa, America and Europe. Importantly, in all of these instances Reesom Haile's poetry has appeared or been heard not only in translation but also in the original Tigrinya and, if in print, in Tigrinya Ge'ez script or, at least, in a Latinized form. Thus, the translation of Tigrinya and its growing audience become a means of preservation for the language itself and – as a medium of profound, local humanism universally reaching out – for our entire, endangered world.

Aiming to enhance and not to endanger the stature of the African language of Tigrinya, the translation of Reesom Haile's poetry still raises the question of the degree to which translations into English can match the style and music of the original. Addressing the literal, oral / aural, literary and poetic sense of the original, and more, impossibilities of translation arise. For example, in the original Tigrinya there is an absolutely daunting abundance of rhyme that would be impossible in English of any period or any serious style, not even in dub or rap. In another respect, the forms or genres of Reesom Haile's poetry have a unique and continuing genesis in Tigrinya and oral culture that most contemporary poetry in English can only palely reflect in writing unless it is appreciated with an informed and acute sense of literary history. For Reesom Haile in his poetry,

The form of the poem is derived from its function. There are forms for work, for praise, for prayer, for bragging, for battle, for joining, weddings, funerals, criticism. My poetry makes use of all these forms, sometimes separately and sometimes in combination. And I have developed new forms for the challenges of building a modern, democratic nation.

The infamous, stinging conundrum of the Italian *traduttore / traditore*, translator / traitor, is at the root of questioning whether translation preserves or endangers mother tongues. The Eritrean conception of the role of the poet is relevant to this problem, particularly in comparison with the European derived formulation of the role of the poet as a "maker," *faber* or *makir*, or as a *vates*, "a prophet," with connections to the spiritual, the underworld, the irrational and the marginal that these terms can connote. Derived from the Tigrinya infinitive *mgTam*, literally *to join*, the Tigrinya word for poetry – *gTmi* that is, "joining," – and the poet – *geTamay*, that is, "joiner" – are comparatively humbler. The Tigrinya terms deflect the more sublime sense of an individual who creates and even speaks for the gods or God. *gTmi* emphasizes a joining of words and worlds from the perspective of the collective, the community, and the society of which the *geTamay* is a part. In oral if not in written form, according to Reesom Haile,

> Poetry is not a special activity of poets, for everyone is a potential a poet. Only that some people are more gifted than others in the art and their words and words more memorable. The poem is not an object separate and apart from its function: to ease the pain and to celebrate the pleasure of life. Women and men alike express themselves in music and poetry while at work or at play.

The poet as "joiner" is like a carpenter or a tinker. Similarly, classical Greek words for "artists" have associations with manufacturing. The word *demiourgos* can be defined as a worker for the people, and the *techne* or art involved can include cooking as well as poetry. *gTmi*,

237

demiourgos or *poietes*, the poet can be a kind of blacksmith: a sense that echoes the role in ancient Greek mythology of Hephaestus making – or *joining*, with gold, silver and less precious metals – the shield of Achilles in *The Iliad*. More humbly, the concept of the poet as a kind of blacksmith evokes a common occupation in Eritrea, where nothing metal is ever wasted but always either repaired or recycled. The Eritrean ability to fashion any spare part imaginable is legendary and has been a matter of necessity. Captured and repaired enemy armaments turned against their original possessors supplied the military hardware for Eritrea's victory in its war for independence. Even today, a visit to Asmara should include its "Medeber" or metal market, where any and all kinds of scrap metal can be seen to metamorphose – in a din of hammering that itself becomes a profound music of drums – into something new and useful: where bomb shells, armored tanks, tire rims, bailing wire, cannons, and rusty mattress springs become buckets, lamps, crutches, chairs, desks, coffee pots, platters, radio spare parts, sledges, axes, shovels and, of course, ploughshares. The seeming madness of Asmara's fleet of 1960s Fiats functioning as the most elegant taxis around the city derives from a method: the ancient and living art of metamorphosis.

Fundamental to poetry, the same process applies to translation, particularly to translation of an African language. There is a common, mistaken assumption that because there are thousands of African languages translating them is quixotic. The impression that there is unique difficulty about Tigrinya and especially its poetry that makes it essentially untranslatable is similarly common, even among many speakers of Tigrinya itself. But guided by the humble conception of *gTmi* or joining – rather than the loftier conceptions of making, creating, and speaking like a prophet – the translator's work can seem a little more, practical, everyday, and honest. Rather than attempting to raise the art of translation into a kind of "transcreation," the joining kind of translation resembles a transmission, with its own special wavelength of poetry itself: a joining translation and metamorphosis of poetry to poetry, poet to poet, primarily and intrinsically themselves as the prelude and the result of the mechanics of literal translation; a process of communication that is a distinct way of thinking in itself, applying the knowledge of two poetry traditions – in this case, Tigrinya and English – and realized in the verbal music or rhythm. It is a universal impulse understood at root with or without translation.

Reesom Haile's poetry also offers a special perspective on two other universal impulses: the political and the religious.

A big reason for the popularity of Reesom Haile's poetry is its political and sometimes impolitic content. He has patriotically rallied his nation any number of times – and there have been many – most famously with his poem "Alewuna, Alewana," "We Have, We Have," a poem so widely and frequently dispersed in Eritrea that the refrain has practically become interchangeable with Reesom Haile's own name. To be anywhere at anytime in Eritrea with Reesom Haile is to hear "Alewuna, Alewana" lovingly pronounced by strangers, young and old, as soon as they recognize his face. Nevertheless, his political role can just as readily turn to that of the poet as defined by Plato's *Republic*: the loyal opposition and, in Lawrence Ferlinghetti's phrase, the "gadfly of the state."

Politically, Reesom Haile is first and foremost a poet of conscience, like all great political poets. Without it, joining poetry and politics only produces propaganda. Furthermore, his poetry ranges freely yet artfully from international to national to local targets: from the politics of bedrooms to the politics of presidential offices. Because he frequently uses allegory, thick and thin, the local can be readily seen as universal and the national as a redemptive paradigm for the international. After all, the use and abuse of power are ubiquitous. Yet everywhere the stakes are high and hotly contested, justifiably so, since the prize is nothing less than individual, national and spiritual survival, as in the poem "Freedom of Speech."

Like animals
People can agree.
But to argue
Seriously or for fun
We have speech.

If we fail
To keep it free,
Not giving everyone,
A say, remember
Babel – it fell.

His strong and prevailing sense of political struggle and ideals might be considered romantic if they were not so realistic and rooted in the unassailable Eritrean political experience of standing alone and winning a 30-year war for independence.

Political poetry in America and Europe is almost an oxymoron – polarizing the many, persuading only the few and nearly always preaching to the converted – though poetry like Amiri Baraka's can be the most accurate political commentary and among the greatest poetry being written in these places today. They could learn a lot from a political art like Reesom Haile's and the way it is comprehensively appreciated from the margins to the center of Eritrean culture and society. In practically every one of his poems, as if he "kept [it] in his stomach along with the food …[he] ate a long time ago," as he has remarked, his political joining is accessible, explicit, tried and true, with the political common sense of a citizen of Eritrea and of the world. He is a poet who is local, national, international and global, and he is patriotic on all accounts. To make or join the language of real political power into a genuine language of poetic power is to humanize the former and popularize the latter towards the betterment of all. There are precedents for proposing such a grand enterprise for poetry, exemplified in the thoroughly political vision Dante's *Divine Comedy* or in Shelley's seeing poets as the "unacknowledged legislators of the world," but Reesom Haile's calling is again rooted in Tigrinya. Signifying "joining" or "poetry," *mgTam* also means to challenge, and the *geTamay*, the poet, by definition is a challenger.

Cultivating the art of political poetry, Reesom Haile's work reveals a similarly unlikely dimension, at least from a contemporary, Euro-American perspective, in being religious and even explicitly biblical or Christian. Explicitly biblical or Christian art in the West today, if not self-critical or, at least, self-conscious, seems hopelessly exclusive and chauvinistic, easily drifting into a form of "hate speech" – a public loss, surely, and a personal loss for many, too. In Reesom Haile's work, however, the biblical framework remains credible and matter of fact, with neither ideology nor inanity. Dozens of his poems illustrate this, like "No Regrets."

> Forget Eden.
> We're not going back.
> Adam and Eve
> Had no regrets.

> "Good riddance,"
> She said.
> "So we were fed.
> He treated us like animals.
> Adam, I love you."

"I love you, too"
He said.
"Nothing beats bread
Baked with your sweat."

Forget Eden.
We're not going back.
Adam and Eve
Had no regrets.

Unlike in most of Africa, Christianity and biblical culture were not imported and imposed by colonialism in the relatively recent history of the region and of Eritrea. Instead, biblical spirituality stems from it through Ge'ez and its language of Tigrinya, as can be similarly said of Egypt, Ethiopia, and countries of the Middle East *and* many of their languages. These are places and languages in which biblical spirituality was born and bred. Their oldest literature includes biblical literature in their own languages. It should be included in a proper anthology of Tigrinya literature, much like an anthology of English literature that includes Anglo-Saxon and Middle English. Moreover, biblical literature is not a bundle of rootless, abstract concepts but existed first and foremost in the original language of its expression, identical with the literary and rhetorical devices of poetry and storytelling, including metaphor, character, plot, setting, suspense, hyperbole, irony, word play, shifting points of view, changing styles, contradiction, endless conflict, song and more. Biblical language – in its oldest texts, alleged originals and best translations – is not a kind of clear container for its ideas. They are inseparable from the language and the style they are expressed in. Sharing the same ancestry, biblical writing and Tigrinya, as exemplified by Reesom Haile's poetry, live on in each other. Their content and style cannot be separated or dissociated. Even when expression in Tigrinya has been Marxist, intent upon its own system of distinguishing between saints and sinners, it is still in a biblical language that will imbue whatever is said because the language is inseparable from its roots if it is to survive *and* thrive. The sacred sense that attaches itself to Jerusalem and Hebrew or Arabic also attaches itself to Asmara, the capital of Eritrea, and to Tigrinya: just as the legend of Sheba, the ancient queen, who bore Solomon's son, Menelik, along a stream near the city, and as he, years later, carried the Ark of the Covenant out of Jerusalem to the same area. Indeed, if "to imagine a language means to imagine a form of life," it must also have memory, ancestors, history, archaeology, myths and a continuing and changing life: precisely as embodied in Reesom Haile's poetry. Questions of theology and belief aside, Christianity and biblical culture are a part of the mother tongue of Tigrinya. In itself and in translation, it not only delights and teaches – the *sine qua non* of literature – but also offers to reconnect us to a past that has been lost and a future with everything to gain.

Reesom Haile is from a family of traditional farmers in Eritrea, where he was born, raised and educated through high school. After working as a radio and television journalist in Ethiopia, he continued his education in the United States. Obtaining a doctorate in Media Ecology from New York University, he served for twenty years as a Development Communications consultant, working with UN Agencies, governments and NGOs around the world before returning to Eritrea in 1994. Since then, he has written over two thousand poems in Tigrinya. His first collection, *waza ms qumneger ntnsae hager* won the 1998 Raimok prize, Eritrea's highest award for literature. His first collection in English was *We Have Our Voice*. Widely published, his poetry has received substantial scholarly and critical attention and extensive media coverage, including *BBC* (UK), *CNN* (USA), *Deutche Welle* (Germany), *RAI* (Italy), *dmtsi Hafash* (Eritrea) *Radio Vatican* (The Vatican), *NPR* (USA), *SABC* (South Africa), *SBS* (Australia) and *VOA* (USA). His performances in Tigrinya and English have inspired audiences throughout Africa, Europe and America.

Charles Cantalupo is a poet, critic, scholar and editor whose writings span the European Renaissance to the African Renaissance. Professor of English, Comparative Literature and African Studies at The Pennsylvania State University and a cultural activist, he organized the international conference and festival, *Against All Odds: African Languages and Literatures into the 21ˢᵗ Century*, held in Asmara, Eritrea, and he was a co-author of the "Asmara Declaration on African Languages and Literatures." His books include *A Literary Leviathan: Thomas Hobbes's Masterpiece of Language, The World of Ngugi wa Thiong'o, Ngugi wa Thiong'o: Texts and Contexts, Anima/l Wo/man and Other Spirits* and, with Reesom Haile, *We Have Our Voice*.